3rd Edition

THE
Morning
Meeting
Book

K–8

Roxann Kriete & Carol Davis

RESPONSIVE CLASSROOM®

The stories in this book are all based on real events in the classroom. However, in order to respect the privacy of students, names and many identifying characteristics of students and situations have been changed.

ISBN: 978-1-892989-60-4

Library of Congress Control Number: 2013957623

Cover and book design adapted for this edition by Helen Merena

Interior photographs © Alice Proujansky, Jeff Woodward, Peter Wrenn, and Vermont Films Group. All rights reserved.

Thanks to the teachers and students who welcomed Northeast Foundation for Children to take photos in their classrooms.

Northeast Foundation for Children, Inc.
85 Avenue A, P.O. Box 718
Turners Falls, MA 01376-0718

800-360-6332
www.responsiveclassroom.org

Second printing 2014

Printed on recycled paper

We would like to thank the Shinnyo-En Foundation for their generous support of the development of this book.

The mission of the Shinnyo-En Foundation is "to bring forth deeper compassion among humankind, to promote greater harmony, and to nurture future generations toward building more caring communities."

A Note From the Editor of the Third Edition

Since its first publication in 1999, *The Morning Meeting Book* has guided teachers in implementing one of the key strategies of the *Responsive Classroom* approach. Over the years, many thousands of teachers have used the wisdom and practical knowledge in this book to help them implement daily Morning Meetings.

The essential practice of Morning Meeting endures but our thinking here at Northeast Foundation for Children about certain aspects of the practice has evolved. Not only have we thought about ways to refine implementation, we've also considered how Morning Meeting fits into today's educational landscape. Because this book is so important to teachers, we wanted to make sure it reflects our most current thinking. With this in mind, we called on Roxann Kriete and Carol Davis to write a third edition of the book.

When a book is co-authored, there's always the challenge of how to address the question of voice. In this case, the structure of the book supported our keeping the authors' individual "I" voices. Roxann wrote the Purposes and Reflections sections of the Overview chapter and each component chapter; the "I" in those sections is Roxann. Carol wrote the Getting Started and Fine Tunings sections of those chapters, and the "I" there is Carol. The conclusion reflects both authors' voices.

What's new in this edition?

The basic structure of the book remains the same but we have integrated upper grades and ELL information into each component chapter; brought the sample greetings, activities, and morning messages into the individual chapters; and added a collection of sharing ideas to try.

Additional changes include:

- Updated information on sharing that addresses around-the-circle and partner sharing as well as dialogue sharing

- Further emphasis on the connections between social-emotional skills and academic learning

- Explanations of how Morning Meeting supports mastery of Common Core State Standards, 21st century skills, and core competencies enumerated by the Collaborative for Academic, Social, and Emotional Learning (CASEL)

- Inclusion of an index

It has been a pleasure to work on this revision with Roxann and Carol and to help ensure that this well-loved book continues to meet the needs of teachers.

Lynn Bechtel
Senior Editor, Northeast Foundation for Children
March 2014

TABLE OF CONTENTS

"It Mattered That I Came"

In the spring of my first year as a secondary school teacher, I got a letter from a student for whom I had a particular fondness, letting me know that she was dropping out of school. School wasn't making much sense to her, and little that she was being asked to learn held much interest for her. She wrote, almost apologetically, that school just wasn't a place where she felt she belonged. More than twenty years later, her words still seem profoundly sad to me:

> I will always remember how you said "Hi, Sue" as I walked into
> eighth period. It made me feel like it really mattered that I came.

It touched and pained me that something that seemed so small to me, an act I hadn't even been aware of, had meant so much to her. I vowed to learn something from it and became more intentional about greeting students. I stationed myself by the door and tried to say a little something to each one as they entered,

1

or at least to make eye contact and smile at every student, not just the ones like Sue for whom I had an instinctive affinity.

Gradually I realized how much I was learning at my post by the door. I observed who bounced in with head up and smile wide, whose eyes were red-rimmed from tears shed in the girls' room at lunch, who mumbled a response into his collar and averted his eyes every day for an entire semester. I didn't know what to do about much of it, but at least I was learning how to notice.

I have learned a lot since then. It is good for students to be noticed, to be seen by their teacher. But it is only a start, not enough by itself. They must notice and be noticed by each other as well.

Years after I taught Sue, I joined the staff of Greenfield Center School, the independent K–8 school founded by Northeast Foundation for Children. There, I saw teachers teaching students to greet each other, to speak to each other, to listen to each other. I saw students start each day together in Morning Meeting where noticing and being noticed were explicit goals.

This book is about Morning Meeting—a particular and deliberate way to begin the school day. Today, many students in K–8 schools around the country launch their school days in Morning Meetings.

In a Morning Meeting, all classroom members—grown-ups and students—gather in a circle, greet each other, and listen and respond to each other's news. We take note of who is present and who is absent; whether it is still raining or not; who is smiling and buoyant; who is having a hard time smiling. We practice academic skills, briefly grapple with problems that challenge our minds, and look forward to the learning we'll do together in the day ahead. Morning Meeting allows us to begin each day as a community of caring and respectful learners.

—Roxann Kriete

MORNING MEETING FORMAT

Morning Meeting lasts up to a half hour each day and is made up of four sequential components: greeting, sharing, group activity, and morning message. The components intentionally provide opportunities for students to practice the skills of greeting, listening and responding, group problem-solving, and noticing and anticipating. Daily practice of the four components gradually weaves a web that binds a class together. Although there is much overlap, each component has its own purposes and structure.

1 *Greeting* ▪ Students greet each other by name, often including handshaking, singing, movement, and other activities.

2 *Sharing* ▪ Students share some news or information about themselves and respond to each other, articulating their thoughts, feelings, and ideas in a positive way.

3 *Group Activity* ▪ The whole class does a short, inclusive activity together, reinforcing learning and building class cohesion through active participation.

4 *Morning Message* ▪ Students practice academic skills and warm up for the day ahead by reading and discussing a daily note to the class posted by their teacher.

Teachers must commit more than just time to implement Morning Meeting successfully. They must also commit themselves to a belief in children's capacity to take care of themselves and each other as they learn academic skills (like vocabulary and algorithms) and social-emotional skills (like respect, responsibility, and stretching the boundaries of their social world). Besides creating opportunities for students to practice such skills, Morning Meeting also creates opportunities for teachers to model these skills and give children valuable feedback.

The time teachers commit to Morning Meeting is an investment that is repaid many times over. The sense of belonging and the skills of attention, listening, expression, and cooperative interaction developed in Morning Meeting are a foundation for every lesson, every transition time, every lining-up, every handling of an upset or conflict, all day and all year long. Morning Meeting is a microcosm of the way we wish our schools to be—communities full of learning, safe and respectful and challenging for all.

THE *RESPONSIVE CLASSROOM*® APPROACH

The Morning Meeting format described in this book was developed by Northeast Foundation for Children as part of the *Responsive Classroom* approach to teaching and learning. Morning Meeting, together with other *Responsive Classroom* practices, gives teachers concrete ways to make academics engaging, manage classrooms effectively, and create a positive climate in which children feel safe to take the risks necessary for learning.

Following are the seven guiding principles of the *Responsive Classroom* approach.

1 The social and emotional curriculum is as important as the academic curriculum.

2 How children learn is as important as what they learn.

3 Great cognitive growth occurs through social interaction.

4 To be successful academically and socially, children need to learn a set of social and emotional skills that include cooperation, assertiveness, responsibility, empathy, and self-control.

5 Knowing the children we teach—individually, culturally, and developmentally—is as important as knowing the content we teach.

6 Knowing the families of the children we teach is as important as knowing the children we teach.

7 How we, the adults at school, work together is as important as our individual competence: Lasting change begins with the adult community.

To learn about other *Responsive Classroom* practices in addition to Morning Meeting, see the resources listed on pages 216–219.

*Morning Meeting gives teachers concrete ways to make
academics engaging, manage classrooms effectively,
and create a positive classroom climate.*

HOW TO USE THIS BOOK

You may choose to read the entire book from beginning to end, select sections that immediately grab your attention, or use the book as a reference as your Morning Meeting experience grows. The book begins with an overview chapter about Morning Meeting as a whole. Next come chapters about each of the four Morning Meeting components, followed by a conclusion.

In the classroom

Each component chapter begins with a section that shows that component in action. Some of these vignettes are from large urban schools; some are from small rural schools. Though the demographics vary widely, the spirit and elements of the Morning Meetings are consistent, the students and their teachers familiar to those of us who spend time in schools. These glimpses take you into the middle of classrooms where Morning Meetings are flourishing.

Purposes and reflections

These sections articulate the purposes and goals of each component and how it fits into the larger context of learning. They highlight and interpret some of the powerful moments created in classrooms and convey some of the specific details and flavor of well-run Morning Meetings.

Getting started

In these sections, you'll find recommendations to help you as you begin to implement the components of Morning Meeting. The suggestions and examples are offered as templates to be used for guidance, not as exact patterns for repetition. Your knowledge of each class's development, pace, and needs—and of your own teaching style—will lead to adaptations that work best for you and the students you teach.

These recommendations are offered with respect for individual teachers and a wish to empower them. They are offered, also, with the awareness, affirmed by thousands of teachers with whom we have worked, that templates drawn by experienced hands are invaluable tools when starting to do something new. Feel free to use these templates—trace them, adapt them, refine them—so that they truly serve you. Just keep the purposes and goals of Morning Meeting in mind as you go.

Each Getting Started section ends with a concise listing of teacher and student responsibilities to help you implement Morning Meeting and assess your practice.

About the Term "Parent"

Students come from a variety of homes with a variety of family structures. Students might be raised by grandparents, siblings, aunts and uncles, foster families, and other caregivers. All of these individuals are to be honored for devoting their time, attention, and love to raising children.

It's difficult to find one word that encompasses all these caregivers. In this book, for ease of reading, we use the term "parent" to represent all the caregivers involved in a child's life.

Fine tunings

The questions and answers in these sections address some concerns and issues teachers commonly encounter as their experience with Morning Meeting evolves. If questions come up for you as you read a chapter or as you use Morning Meeting, look in the chapter's Fine Tunings section for help. Also check out the other Morning Meeting resources listed on pages 216–219 and at www.responsiveclassroom.org.

Ideas for greeting, sharing, group activity, morning message

We've included ideas for each component. You can use these ideas as written, adapt them to meet the needs of the students you teach, or use them as a spring-board for creating your own ideas. These ideas cover grades K–8 and address a range of academic and social-emotional learning goals.

Morning Meeting

AN OVERVIEW

It's almost 8:30 on a winter morning and students from the last-to-arrive bus are entering the classroom, hanging their coats, and reading the morning message that their teacher, Ms. Suretti, has written to them. Students who arrived earlier are working at a variety of tasks: some are writing entries in their journals; some are at computer stations practicing math facts; some are quizzing each other on the week's spelling words.

Ms. Suretti turns from her post near the door where she has been greeting students, picks up a chime from the bookshelf nearby, and strikes it gently with a mallet. When the quiet hum in the room has turned to silence and everyone's eyes are on her, she says, "It's Morning Meeting time. Put away what you are working on and come to the rug."

Students and teachers crave a certain amount of predictability and routine in the school day, especially at the start of the day. The format of Morning Meeting provides this predictability while allowing room for variation and change. Meetings reflect the style and flavor of individual teachers and groups. They also reflect the ebb and flow of a school year's seasons—August's new supplies and anxious, careful faces; December's pre-vacation excitement; February's endless colds and coughs; April's spring-has-sprung exuberance. The mixture of routine and surprise, of comfort and challenge, makes Morning Meeting a treasured and flexible teaching tool.

PURPOSES AND REFLECTIONS

Our increasingly global 21st century society, marked by rapid innovation and change, has engendered widespread acknowledgment that students need, more than ever, to develop strong cognitive abilities and social and emotional proficiencies. Morning Meetings nurture and provide a place to practice all of these skills.

Among the competencies needed for success in the 21st century are the abilities to communicate ideas and information clearly; to collaborate; to demonstrate innovation and think flexibly; and to analyze, synthesize, and evaluate information from diverse sources. The importance of these skills is highlighted by widespread adoption of the Common Core State Standards, which emphasize teaching these very thinking, speaking, and listening competencies.

Of equal importance are the skills of responsible citizenship. The world we live in requires citizens who can learn from and work collaboratively with others from diverse cultures (Bellanca & Brandt, 2010; Partnership for 21st Century Skills, n.d.). Strong communication and cross-cultural skills are essential for this.

Threaded through our common understanding of the need for these competencies is a growing sense of the value of social-emotional skills. The Collaborative for Academic, Social, and Emotional Learning (CASEL), a leading organization in the field of education, describes social and emotional learning (SEL) as helping children develop skills that are important for success in school and in life. These skills include recognizing and managing emotions, developing caring and concern and showing understanding and empathy for others, establishing positive relationships, making responsible decisions, and handling challenging situations constructively (CASEL, n.d.).

Research confirms the long-held conviction of many educators regarding the critical importance of these social-emotional skills and their connection to academic progress. Recently, a group of researchers analyzed over 200 studies and found that students who receive SEL instruction had more positive attitudes about school and improved an average of eleven percentile points on standardized achievement tests compared to students who did not receive such instruction (Durlack, Dymnicki, Schellinger, Taylor, and Weissberg, 2011).

A person who can demonstrate self-control and listen well, who can frame a thoughtful question and pose it respectfully, and who can examine a situation from a number of perspectives will be a stronger learner. All those skills—so essential to academic achievement—can be modeled, experienced, practiced, extended, and refined in the context of social interaction. And Morning Meeting provides a forum in which this integration of social interaction and skill development can occur.

The Morning Meeting components also offer students endless opportunities to practice academic skills—whether counting by 2s, using vocabulary words correctly, or reviewing newly learned geology concepts—in a safe and energizing way.

Overview

Purposes of Morning Meeting

- Sets a tone for respectful and engaged learning in a climate of trust

- Builds and enhances connections among students and between students and teachers

- Merges academic, social, and emotional learning

- Motivates students by addressing the human need to feel a sense of significance and belonging, and to have fun

- Through the repetition of many ordinary moments of respectful interaction, enables some extraordinary moments

Morning Meeting sets a tone for respectful and engaged learning in a climate of trust

Beginnings can be critical. The leader of a workshop I once attended asked our group of teachers and principals to recall and describe our first half hour as teachers. Every one of us, even those whose first teaching moments had happened thirty years earlier, could recall in vivid detail what happened and how we felt in those first thirty minutes.

Certainly, the first thirty minutes of each day are not as embedded in memory as the first thirty minutes in a new career. On some days, in fact, we can hardly remember at 4:00 in the afternoon what happened at 9:00 that morning. However, while the details may have flown our cluttered memory, the pace and flavor of our first half hour in school likely influenced the way we felt at the end of the day and whether the day's challenges had been exhilarating or overwhelming. The same is true for our students: Beginnings matter.

The way we begin each day in our classroom sets the tone for learning and speaks volumes about what and whom we value, about our expectations for the way we will treat each other, and about the way we believe learning occurs.

Students' learning begins the second they walk through the doors of the building. Children notice whether they are greeted warmly or overlooked, whether the classroom feels chaotic and unpredictable or ordered and comforting. If they announce, "My cat got hit by a car last night but it's gonna be all right," they may find an interested, supportive audience or one that turns away. Every detail of their experience informs students about the classroom and their place in it.

When we start the day with everyone together, face to face, welcoming each person, sharing news, listening to individual voices, and communicating as a caring group, we make several powerful statements. We say that every person counts. We say that the way we interact individually and as a group is significant. We say that our classroom culture is one of friendliness and thoughtfulness. We say that we can accomplish hard work and make important discoveries together. We say that teachers hold authority, even though they are a part of the circle. We say that

Morning Meeting helps to create a climate of trust that encourages children to take risks.

this is a place where courtesy and warmth and safety reign—a place of respect for all.

To learn, we must take risks—offering up a tentative answer we are far from sure is right, or trying out a new part in the chorus when we are not sure we can hit the notes. We are more willing to take these risks when we know we will be respected and valued, no matter the outcome. To risk, we must trust, and Morning Meeting helps create a climate of trust.

When we hold Morning Meetings consistently over time, we see the friendly, respectful behaviors established in the circle overflow beyond it. We overhear students talking at lunch about a common interest discovered during a Morning Meeting sharing, forging the beginning of a new friendship. Children may start to greet each other spontaneously at the start of the day, even before Morning Meeting begins.

A first grade teacher whose class had been using Morning Meeting for several months wrote: "One Tuesday as I stood by the door, waiting for the class to gather, I just watched. They were genuinely glad to see each other. Some were hugging as they greeted each other. Some were clapping for something. What a joy to watch—I was merely an observer and just loved it."

Morning Meeting provides an anchor for older students

For students between the ages of ten and fourteen, the consistency of regular Morning Meetings may be especially important. It can provide an anchor at a time of rapid physical and emotional changes. Students this age are coming into the full power of their personalities and intellect. This is a critical age for practicing and developing the relationship and work skills that will serve them well in adult life. However, just when they are becoming capable of abstract, theoretical thinking—and of higher level moral thinking—they also become emotionally volatile, pre-occupied with physical changes, and immersed in a peer culture that often says it's cool to be "bad" and uncool to be smart. All these happenings can impede intellectual and personal growth and achievement.

More than ever in their lives, these students need a predictable routine that helps them trust each other and value learning. Morning Meeting "offers an alternative to the dog-eat-dog world that many kids live in," says Barbara Forshag, a middle school educator from Louisiana. "[It] offers them another way to be." Beginning the day with Morning Meeting is an important step toward making school a safe and productive place for learners of all ages.

Morning Meeting builds and enhances connections among students and between students and teachers

Feeling connected to a school community is an important factor in students' success. Students who feel connected to school report that they like school, feel they belong, have friends at school, and believe their teachers care about them and their learning. Attendance improves along with students' motivation and engagement with learning (Blum, 2005).

Morning Meeting helps to create and extend connections among all members of the classroom community. Each component helps children to know others and to be known. Greeting, for example, begins with the very basic element of learning and using each other's names. Sharing helps students learn details about each other's experiences, preferences, and interests, as well as those of their teachers. Picture Kezziah, who loves knowing that her teacher, Mr. Russell, likes snakes too and has a pet boa constrictor. Or imagine the connections that form when a query the teacher has embedded in the morning message prompts students to gather and graph information about how many siblings they have. Reading the message, Jeremy learns that Gavin is an identical twin too. All these personal connections can help children feel acknowledged and motivated to learn.

The opportunity for positive connection that Morning Meeting provides is just as important in the upper grades as the lower ones. Pre-adolescence and adolescence are marked by tumultuous emotional, physical, and cognitive changes. Morning Meeting enables students this age to do what they most want and need to do: interact with their peers.

Older students long to be part of the group, but they're often not quite sure how to join together in a way that doesn't exclude others. The four components of Morning Meeting allow students to connect with their peers in a safe, positive, and inclusive way. Through the structures of Morning Meeting they can learn how to turn their need for peer connection into a positive and dynamic learning strategy.

In addition to helping individuals within the classroom community know each other better, Morning Meetings help build cultural knowledge and appreciation. Each classroom represents a unique community of students and families, and Morning Meeting offers many ways that we can take advantage of the diversity inherent in every group. We can help the class to learn and use greetings in different languages and in the process make connections to various students' family origins. Topics for sharing can include information about families' favorite foods, games, and traditions. Sometimes games that are shared can become group activities. Cross-cultural understanding and competence develops as students share information from their own lives and learn about those of their classmates.

Finally, observing and interacting with students in Morning Meetings give teachers an opportunity to garner important information that can help them differentiate instruction to respond to the needs and strengths of individual students. For example, what we learn in Morning Meeting can help as we choose books that might capture a reluctant reader's interests or assign partners for a science project.

Morning Meeting merges academic, social, and emotional learning

Morning Meeting provides ample daily opportunities for children to review information learned in content areas and practice skills specific to those areas. For example, an activity might draw on recently learned math skills or a morning message may ask children to correct capitalization errors.

But perhaps more importantly, the respectful, inclusive setting of Morning Meeting harnesses the innate synergy among academic, social, and emotional learning. As social beings, we learn through dialogue with others—and this is true no matter what the subject matter. We extend our knowledge, test our assumptions, confirm or revise our thoughts, and generate questions that will lead to a new iteration of ideas. Knowing how to observe and reflect, to speak and to listen is fundamental to our ability to learn. These skills enable us to exchange perspectives and ideas, explain our thinking, and critique the thinking of others—skills that children need for success in all areas of school and of life.

Increasingly, people are acknowledging the role that dialogue plays in promoting academic growth. As one example, the Common Core State Standards (CCSS) place a strong emphasis on speaking and listening skills. The speaking and listening standards state directly that students should "prepare for and participate effectively in a range of conversations and collaborations with diverse partners" and note that "in order to build a foundation for college and career readiness, students must have ample opportunities to take part in a variety of rich, structured conversations—as part of a whole class, in small groups, and with a partner" (Common Core State Standards Initiative, 2012).

Morning Meeting provides a daily arena for "rich, structured conversations" in which social, emotional, and academic learning is an integrated experience, full of chances to develop foundational thinking and language skills such as listening attentively, speaking clearly, asking purposeful questions, answering thoughtfully, giving reasons for assertions, and agreeing and disagreeing respectfully.

A group activity—Mystery Word (page 162)—from a lively Morning Meeting in Ms. Franklin's second grade classroom provides a great example.

> "Our activity today is Mystery Word," Ms. Franklin announces. The students lean forward eagerly as she holds up a handful of neatly lettered oak tag cards she has prepared. Each tag has on it one word from an article titled "Superstorms" that the class had read the previous day. A tornado, rare in their area, had touched down in a neighboring town a few months earlier, affecting many people they knew, and students' interest in the topic is keen. After quickly summarizing the article with the class, reviewing some key details, and confirming that everyone is familiar with the words on the cards, Ms. Franklin says to the class, "Ready to start? Isaiah, your turn to go first."
>
> As Isaiah stands and closes his eyes, Ms. Franklin makes a show of shuffling the cards and then tapes one to his back. Slowly, with his back turned to his classmates to display his mystery word, he sidles around the inside of the circle. His classmates will offer clues to him—"in complete sentences," reminds their teacher—until he guesses the word correctly.
>
> "When the tornado came, it blanked a lot of trees," the first clue-giver says.
>
> "Destroyed?" Isaiah guesses.
>
> "Well, that would work, but it's not the word."
>
> "Sometimes when a tree gets blanked it doesn't live anymore," comes the next clue.
>
> Isaiah stands, thinking hard. "Uh, uprooted?"
>
> A resounding "Yes!" from the whole circle celebrates his response and Round Two begins.

Overview

This activity was rich with the reinforcement of academic content and practice in listening and speaking skills. Students used content vocabulary; followed directions; took turns; practiced patient, respectful listening; used complete sentences; and delighted in each other's success. The article and its vocabulary would be fresh in their minds later in the day when they began writing stories connected to the topic. This conversation and activity sharpened the tools of listening and speaking that are essential for partner chats, small group discussions, peer critiquing, and other cooperative learning strategies. The preamble and the activity itself took perhaps ten minutes: ten precious minutes of rapt engagement with the curriculum and each other.

Morning Meeting motivates students by addressing the human need to feel a sense of significance and belonging, and to have fun

All of us need to feel that we belong and are valued for the competencies, skills, and knowledge we bring to a group. We need to feel that our unique contributions are recognized and appreciated. All the components of Morning Meeting address those needs directly.

Educational consultant Melissa Correa-Connolly speaks of what she has seen happen, both in her own classroom and in the rooms of many teachers with whom she has worked:

> I think of Morning Meeting as having such immense power because it meets the emotional needs of children. It acknowledges everyone and makes them feel significant. It does away with the feeling many children have of being a piece of furniture in the classroom. Morning Meeting is the first thing in the morning and it allows children to be seen and to have a voice.

Having fun is also a universal human need. Fun does not necessarily mean frivolity or silliness; it does mean engagement and fascination with what we do. An activity can be fun and playful even when it's hard and the challenge great. Having fun is not about winning, but about immersion in the pleasure of the activity itself.

*Morning Meeting is full of opportunities to practice academic
and social skills while having fun together.*

Fun might involve striving to find the five punctuation errors planted in the morning message or learning to sing a song in three-part harmony. It might mean trying to guess the three-digit number a classmate is thinking of in the game Pica Fermé Nada (page 164). Fun might mean learning a new and lively greeting E.J. brought back from summer camp or laughing along with Amy when she reports on her new puppy's antics. Fun is also connected with risk-taking. Risks taken in a playful way can teach us how to handle the more serious risks that growth can demand.

One thing is certain. Humans strive to fulfill their needs in whatever way they can, whether those ways are positive or negative. The student who isn't recognized in the group for friendly contributions may become known for his trouble-making contributions. When school doesn't provide constructive ways to meet students' needs for fun, students may devise their own, often not-so-constructive or inclusive ways.

Morning Meeting is full of opportunities for a class to have fun together and for all its members to feel a sense of significance and belonging, needs affirmed by theory and research: "Adler (1930) proposed that a sense of belonging motivates children to develop their skills and contribute to the welfare of all.... Research indicates that educators who establish firm boundaries, foster warm personal relationships in the classroom, and enable students to have an impact on their environment strengthen students' attachment to their school, their interest in learning, their ability to refrain from self-destructive behaviors, and their positive behaviors" (Elias et al., 1997, p. 44).

Through the repetition of many ordinary moments of respectful interaction, Morning Meeting enables some extraordinary moments

Morning Meeting, repeated every day, is full of moments that by themselves may seem quite mundane. But this repetition can enable some quite extraordinary moments within the meeting circle. For example, the habits of participation established by Morning Meeting routines can serve a community well in very difficult circumstances. Teacher Joyce Love's experience testifies to this.

By taking part in Morning Meeting, her class had learned how to come quickly together and how to listen respectfully to each other. They had considered hard questions, such as "What can you say when someone shares something that's really upsetting to them?" as well as "What might we say when someone shares something that makes them really happy?" They had, under Joyce's guidance, carefully constructed habits of participation and practiced them day in and day out in the most ordinary situations with the most ordinary news—a swimming test passed, a baby brother with chicken pox, a visit from relatives.

One morning, several of Joyce's students saw a dead body on a street corner on their walk to school. Now, when they were confronted with an event of monumental impact, they had a familiar circle to come to. They had patterns of sharing and response that their teacher could draw on to help them deal with a haunting scene.

The predictable format of Morning Meeting provides stability and comfort.

"If it hadn't been for Morning Meeting, I wouldn't have known what to do," Joyce recalled. "Its structures helped take care of things."

Morning Meetings also help when students are affected by the news of difficult events that have occurred in the larger world, whether it's an earthquake that left thousands homeless or a bomb blast that killed many. The established, predictable format of the meeting is familiar and comforting during disturbing times. In addition, having all students gathered in a circle allows the teacher to notice any whose distress seems acute and who might need extra attention or support beyond the classroom. And perhaps most importantly, the very restoration of routine sends a powerful message that helps to model and build resilience: Hard things happen, we acknowledge them, and we continue on.

Thankfully, not all extraordinary moments are tragic ones. Consider this story told by a teacher from a school where Morning Meetings were an established part of school life in all the classrooms:

> One wintry Tuesday morning at about 9:30, just as Morning Meeting in my room was ending, a second grader from the classroom adjacent to mine entered and approached me politely. "Excuse me, Mrs. Truesdell,

but our teacher isn't here yet. We finished Morning Meeting, but we don't know what to do next."

A series of missed communications involving a school secretary with the flu and a faulty answering machine had resulted in a class without a teacher or a substitute. These seven-year-olds knew the routines so well that they had gathered themselves and conducted an orderly and merry Morning Meeting. I remembered, in fact, hearing the strains of the song "River" wafting through the thin wall that connected the two rooms and thinking how much better it sounded than last week!

These children's daily participation in the ongoing routines of Morning Meeting had enabled them to take responsibility for these routines even in the absence of their teacher. Their school celebrated their responsible behavior at an assembly later that week.

GETTING STARTED

Establish a set schedule for Morning Meeting

Ideally, Morning Meeting happens every day, first thing in the morning. The length of the meeting is important—plan on twenty to thirty minutes. If the meeting is much shorter than twenty minutes, achieving the desired social-emotional and academic goals is difficult. If the meeting is too long, students become restless and the meeting loses impact.

Of course, a Morning Meeting may need to be shorter than twenty minutes on days with special events such as field trips, guest speakers, or school assemblies. You might do all four components but keep each one brief. Alternatively, you could do just two components, such as a greeting and the message. This would maintain the routine and set the tone for the day.

When students change classes

In many schools, upper elementary grades begin the structure of changing classes a few times a day. Finding time to schedule Morning Meeting can be challenging in these situations. If possible, collaborate with team members and other colleagues to find an optimal solution.

Here are some ideas:

- *Do Morning Meeting three times a week during advisory or homeroom.* Much of the benefit of Morning Meeting comes from repeated practice of social-emotional and academic skills. If Morning Meeting is only an occasional event, not only is its impact diminished, but it's also likely that the meeting itself will be less successful, since students won't have developed the skills necessary for a productive meeting. It's important, therefore, to schedule Morning Meetings several times a week and as much as possible on the same days, so that students have a predictable structure to look forward to.

  On days when you don't do a full Morning Meeting, you might do two components—perhaps greeting and morning message. Or you might plan advisory or homeroom activities that reinforce skills such as respectful listening and questioning, self-control, focused presentation, and cooperative learning. For example, you could schedule peer tutoring, service learning projects, or team-building activities.

- *Do portions of Morning Meeting at other times of the day.* If you need to do an abbreviated Morning Meeting first thing in the morning, you could incorporate the missed portions into other parts of the day. For example, you could do sharing as an energizer during an academic lesson, after silent reading, or at closing circle at the end of the day.

- *Do all of Morning Meeting at a different time of day.* Although it's best if Morning Meeting comes at the beginning of the day, it's not always possible. Some schools have advisory during second period. In that case, that's when Morning Meeting might take place. If your school doesn't have an advisory or homeroom period, you may have to look for a consistent segment of time such as a sustained silent reading or study hall.

Consider the space and setup for the meeting

One of the first things to think about when planning for Morning Meetings is the space where you'll hold them. You'll want to create a space large enough for all participants to sit in an even circle so that all can see and be seen—this is an essential element of the meeting. Many teachers set this space off with a colorful carpet or carpet squares to indicate, "This is our gathering spot."

Creating this space can present challenges in small or oddly shaped classrooms, but it's worth persevering. Holding Morning Meetings in an elongated oval or amoeba shape can result in some students feeling unnoticed and disengaged and work against one of the purposes of Morning Meeting, which is to welcome all into the classroom and build community. Sometimes having a colleague look at your space with you can be helpful—a fresh set of eyes might see ways you can reconfigure the space. (For ideas on creating meeting spaces, see the *What Every Teacher Needs to Know* K–5 book series by Mike Anderson and Margaret Berry Wilson, published by Northeast Foundation for Children.)

You'll also want to think about whether students will sit on the floor or in chairs. Your decision will depend partly on students' developmental needs. Many students sit quite happily on the floor; others seem to handle themselves better, or feel recognized as being more mature, when seated in chairs. Some students simply need the physical support of chairs. When I taught fifth graders, we began the year sitting on the floor for Morning Meeting, and I had to repeatedly remind them to sit up. I soon realized that they were going through tremendous growth spurts and were physically uncomfortable on the floor. A quick switch to chairs remedied the situation.

Lay the groundwork for Morning Meeting

In the first days of school, it's important to spend some time helping students get ready for successful participation in Morning Meeting. This preparation includes

The teacher uses the hands-up signal to ask for the group's attention simply, effectively, and respectfully.

teaching a signal for quiet, teaching and modeling basic routines such as how to come to the meeting circle, briefly introducing the purpose of Morning Meeting, and presenting or creating meeting rules. Laying this groundwork doesn't take a lot of time and is a crucial step for ongoing success with Morning Meeting. In the following sections you'll find "how-to" information on each of these topics.

Choose and teach signals you will use consistently

Having simple, effective signals to get students' attention is essential. Raising your voice may be simple but is rarely effective, and if students are involved in conversations or activities, chances are that many will not absorb the announcement.

Instead, you can use various nonverbal signals that say to students, "Stop what you are doing and give me [or a student who may be about to speak] your attention." To call students to the meeting circle, an auditory signal such as a chime, bell, or triangle or a visual signal such as dimming the lights might be most effective. When you have the attention of all students, make a brief statement. "Five minutes till Morning Meeting. Put away what you are working on and come to the meeting area."

When students are gathered in the meeting circle, a hands-up signal is useful to get their quiet attention. Suppose it is Jonas's turn to share. He has brought a picture of his new hamster, Harry, but has left it in his desk. When Jonas leaves the circle to get the picture, his classmates start chatting. Jonas comes back, ready to share, but his classmates continue to talk. The teacher, Mrs. Regules, raises her hand. Across the circle, Amanda notices and raises hers. Around the circle hands go up as the signal spreads and silence follows. It is simple and efficient, with not a word of scolding or blame. His audience is ready, and Jonas begins. "This is a picture of Harry. He's really a she . . ."

Carefully teach routines

Over and over in our teaching lives, we are reminded not to make assumptions about what students know. This applies to daily classroom routines just as it applies to academic content. Many routines contribute to smoothly running Morning Meetings. Perhaps you'll want everyone to bring chairs to the circle, or move furniture around to create room for a circle. Once in the circle, students need to know how to sit with empty, quiet hands, and how to listen attentively. Plus, each component of Morning Meeting has its own routines—how to greet someone respectfully, how to share information, how to move safely during an activity. These routines require careful instruction at the outset and vigilant monitoring even after they have been established.

Use Interactive Modeling to teach routines

Interactive Modeling is a useful strategy for teaching Morning Meeting routines. Interactive Modeling starts with the teacher modeling a desired action or behavior but extends beyond that. It actively involves students in noticing and naming the modeled behavior and then in practicing the behavior while the teacher watches and gives feedback. These extra steps help students better grasp and remember new routines.

Here are the steps of Interactive Modeling and what they look like when Mr. Barnes uses them to teach the class how to move their chairs to Morning Meeting.

2

Interactive Modeling: How to Move Chairs to Morning Meeting

1	*Say what you will model and why.*	Mr. Barnes: "In order to have enough time for our Morning Meeting, we need to efficiently move chairs into the meeting circle—and we need to do it in a safe way so we take care of our classroom and each other. Notice what it looks like and sounds like when I move my chair."
2	*Model the behavior.*	Mr. Barnes puts both hands on the back of a chair and carries it with legs pointing down. When he gets to the meeting circle, he gently places the chair on the floor.
3	*Ask students what they noticed.*	Mr. Barnes: "What did I do that was safe and efficient?" The children name several things: He used two hands, he kept the chair in front of him, he watched where he was going so he wouldn't bump into anyone, he set the chair down quietly.
4	*Invite one or more students to model.*	Mr. Barnes: "Who else can show us how to carry a chair safely and efficiently just like I did?" He calls on Shante and says to the class, "Watch carefully and see what you notice."
5	*Again, ask students what they noticed.*	Mr. Barnes: "What did Shante do that was safe and efficient?" Children again point out details.
6	*Have all students practice.*	Mr. Barnes: "Now we're all going to practice. When I call your table group, pick up your chair and move to the circle the way you saw demonstrated."
7	*Provide feedback.*	Mr. Barnes: "All of you remembered to keep two hands on the chair with the legs down. I also noticed you went directly to the meeting circle without stopping to chat with your friends. That will really help us to get to meeting safely and efficiently so we have time to do our entire Morning Meeting."

After this kind of formal, structured practice, many teachers deliberately cue students to put the behaviors into action during real classroom work while they observe and coach. For example, after the formal practice described above, Mr. Barnes says, "Tomorrow, as you finish your morning jobs, you will need to bring your chair to Morning Meeting by 9:05. You'll have another chance to practice bringing your chair safely and efficiently." Then, right before the actual meeting, he reminds the group, "Think about how you will carry your chair so that you are both safe and efficient."

(For more on Interactive Modeling, see *Interactive Modeling: A Powerful Technique for Teaching Children* by Margaret Berry Wilson, published by Northeast Foundation for Children.)

Introduce Morning Meeting to students

If students are new to Morning Meeting, begin by establishing their prior knowledge about meetings. You might ask, "What are some kinds of meetings you know about—meetings that you, your parents, or someone you know have been to? What kinds of things happened at those meetings?" After students share their ideas and experiences, let them know that they'll begin each day with a meeting called Morning Meeting. Describe the meeting and tell them your hopes and goals for this part of the day. Your list might sound something like this:

- I hope that we will all get to know one another—not just our best friends or the people we hang out with all of the time—so that everyone will feel that they're part of our classroom community.
- I want us to be able to share different experiences and ideas.
- I want us to learn and have fun together as a group.

If students are already familiar with Morning Meeting from previous years, ask them to name their hopes and goals for this part of the day.

Often, teachers of older students worry that Morning Meeting may seem babyish, particularly if students remember doing it in first and second grade. Emphasize the amount of peer interaction that will occur during Morning Meeting—something that older students crave as their peer group becomes more and more important. And reassure them that you will plan meetings that reflect their interests and draw from their curriculum. Your enthusiastic introduction of Morning Meeting and careful planning can go a long way toward making Morning Meeting a success for these students.

Establish Morning Meeting ground rules

From the very beginning, it is important to establish some ground rules and procedures that will help Morning Meeting run smoothly. These can be teacher generated or created collaboratively with the class. In either case, the ground rules should be few in number and stated positively—these rules are helpful guideposts for behavior, not harsh prohibitions.

If you choose to work with the students to create meeting rules, begin the process with a question such as "To make our Morning Meeting respectful, safe, and fun, what rules will we need?" This question helps students stay focused on the purpose of rules—to maintain safety and order for all.

Answers will likely include some variation of the following:

- Listen respectfully
- Look at the person who's talking
- Keep your body in control
- Raise your hand if you want to talk
- Keep your hand down when someone is speaking
- Make room for everyone in the circle
- Offer thoughtful questions and comments

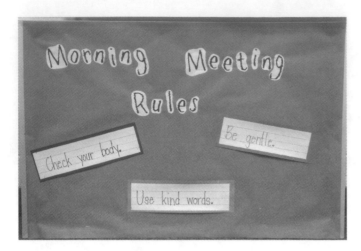

Meeting rules vary depending on the age and needs of a group. The rules on the left were created with kindergartners, those on the right with a class of fourth graders.

Because a long list of rules can be difficult to follow, edit this list down to three to five essential rules that encompass all the details named. Give students a helpful reminder by posting the rules near the Morning Meeting space.

With both teacher-created and co-created rules, it's important to discuss and model the rules over the first few weeks of doing Morning Meetings so that students have a concrete understanding of what following the rules looks like and sounds like.

In a seventh grade class, the teacher leads a discussion of what it means to "be respectful." "How do people show respect in a meeting?" she asks. In a kindergarten class, one of the meeting rules is "Listen to each other." "How will someone who's speaking know that you're listening?" the teacher asks. In both classrooms, discussions ensue on the finer points of listening etiquette and respectful meeting behavior. Each teacher then uses Interactive Modeling, as described on pages 26–27, to demonstrate and have students practice these behaviors.

Start with simple Morning Meetings and increase complexity over time

Many teachers, particularly those of older students, find that they can successfully do a complete but simple Morning Meeting on the first day of school. Others might just do a greeting on the first day, and phase in the other components over the next few days. The goal is to do all four components as soon as students are ready. Factors such as the students' age and school experience and your knowledge of the particular group of students you're teaching will influence how quickly you phase in components.

In the early days of school, keep all components simple, highly structured, and low risk, even in classrooms where students are familiar with Morning Meeting from previous years. Choose greetings and activities that are straightforward and easy to manage, carefully structure sharing, and focus your message on one task. For example, in a first Morning Meeting with fourth graders, you might do an Interview Greeting (page 78), which combines greeting and sharing, followed by Take Sides (page 166) for the group activity and end with a simple message to get students thinking about what they are looking forward to in fourth grade.

Overview

As a sense of positive community gets established and students get to know each other better, you can introduce more high-risk elements. Of course, what feels risky can change throughout the year depending on emerging issues, events, or developmental needs. (For more information about increasing the complexity of individual components, see the Getting Started sections in the chapters that follow.)

Do the four components in order

The order of the four components—greeting, sharing, group activity, and morning message—matters. Once you've taught all four components, stick to this order. Greeting serves as a logical warm-up and tone-setter for sharing, which requires that students feel a sense of comfort and trust in the group. For sharing to work well, the group must be feeling settled and calm. When teachers try doing sharing after group activity, they often notice that the students aren't able to listen well or ask focused and thoughtful questions.

Group activity follows sharing because at this point in the meeting the children are ready for the invigoration of whole-group involvement. Morning message helps to bring the group back to a calmer mood after the liveliness of activity and serves as a transition to the rest of the school day.

Plan meetings purposefully

A rich and meaningful Morning Meeting does not happen by accident. Just as with lessons, a teacher needs to plan Morning Meetings purposefully, considering several factors.

How much time do you have for the meeting?

Determine how much time you have for Morning Meeting on a given day and choose ideas for each component accordingly. If you choose a longer greeting and activity, choose a shorter sharing and message so that everything fits into your twenty- to thirty-minute time frame.

How can you incorporate elements from the curriculum?

Figure out ways to integrate skills, concepts, and ideas from the academic curriculum into the meetings. For example, for a third grade language arts class beginning a unit on mysteries, you might choose Alibi (page 154) as a group activity. This game would give students a fun way to use key vocabulary from the unit. For sixth graders who are studying energy in science class, you could do an around-the-circle sharing about a recent time when students noticed energy in use. Students could then sort the examples into categories of different kinds of energy.

What social-emotional skills do students need to practice?

What are students' social-emotional strengths and challenges? Where are they in their development? What are some recent challenges that they would benefit

*Partner sharing helps children practice
respectful listening.*

from working on? Consider these questions as you plan your Morning Meeting. For example, a sixth grade teacher observed the formation of cliques and knew that some students were feeling excluded at various times during the day. As part of her effort to address this, she decided to focus on team building in the next Morning Meeting and chose a greeting, sharing, and activity that had students interact with many different classmates.

What's the mood of the class?

Finally, gauge the class's mood. Are they preoccupied by certain current events? Is a holiday affecting their ability to focus? Sometimes these are things you can plan for. For example, on the morning after Halloween, the selected content and structure of the meeting may need to be low-key and calming. You might plan in advance to use a simple seated greeting and a focused partner share on "What I did last night."

At other times, you may need to make a quick change to the meeting after assessing students as they walk through the door. For example, on a gray Monday morning when students seem sleepy, you may need to select more invigorating content, like the One-Minute Greeting (page 79) and a round of Aroostasha (page 154) for the group activity. The key is to know the students you teach, plan accordingly, observe, and adjust if needed on the spot (something you'll get better at, with practice!).

Morning Meetings are rich with opportunities
for students to engage with academic content.

Planning pays off

The thought of planning for yet another "subject" may seem overwhelming. I can remember feeling that way when I first began implementing Morning Meeting. "I hardly have enough time to plan for the core subjects that I'm required to teach," I lamented to my fourth grade teaching partner. But as she and I planned together, we began to discover ways to integrate the curriculum into Morning Meetings. We also created simple planning sheets that directed our thinking and kept us focused on both the goals of Morning Meeting and the life of the classroom, all while keeping the meetings to twenty or thirty minutes. As the year progressed, Morning Meetings became an essential part of the day, rich with opportunities for academic engagement and community building.

Take charge of the flow and dynamics of each meeting

Make no mistake: Successful Morning Meetings require a teacher who is in control. As teachers we are planners, interpreters, synthesizers, timekeepers, and safety-net holders. Just as we are in charge of lessons in social studies, math, or language arts, we need to stay in charge of running Morning Meetings.

What is required of us in this role may be simple and straightforward. "Choose one more person for a question or comment, Danita," we say when many hands are raised and time is running short; "Join the circle, Todd," to a student who tends to hang back.

Other times, discerning and guiding the dynamics in Morning Meeting can be more complex. Eleven-year-old Jeremy continually shares complicated details of "scary science" stories about mutant viruses, colliding asteroids, and toxic pesticides that invisibly saturate strawberries. He is highly knowledgeable and his graphic details are accurate and documented.

Jeremy's teacher wonders about the effect of this stream of threatening news, so authoritatively presented, on his peers. Are they upset, challenged, or embarrassed by their relative lack of factual knowledge? Is this a positive way for Jeremy to define a niche in the class? Careful observation and perhaps a one-on-one chat with Jeremy outside of Morning Meeting will inform his teacher as she contemplates whether her intervention is needed to protect either him or the class.

Hold students to meeting rules and expectations

Addressing what can seem like small details—whom students greet, where they sit, which students are rarely the recipients of thoughtful comments—sends two messages: You value the skills and attitudes that specific actions reflect, and you believe in the students' capacity to accomplish these actions.

Let students know by your comments that you notice how they are doing with the named expectations and that you will hold them to those expectations—and support them with reminders and directions when needed. Frame your comments in the positive, focusing on what students are doing well or on helping them identify what would be a better way, rather than naming what they are not doing well.

Think of these sorts of comments as the "three R's"—reinforcing, reminding, and redirecting. Following are some examples.

Reinforcing

- Lots of people are choosing to sit next to different classmates today.

- I notice the way everyone remembered to smile at the person they greeted today.

- Most people are remembering to read the message chart when they enter our room in the morning.

- You are giving many specific details to support your ideas in sharing.

Reminding

- Laurie, what do you need to remember as you move your chair into the circle?

- What things do you need to remember so everyone feels safe to share their ideas during this activity?

- Meeting rules, everyone.

- What will we need to keep in mind if someone makes a mistake during this activity?

Redirecting

- Eyes on the speaker, Natalie.

- Hands down until the speaker is finished.

- Mateo, keep your body in your own space.

- Laurie, you need to walk in this activity.

Give students responsibility in Morning Meeting

Virtually every moment in Morning Meeting is laden with opportunities for students to assume responsibility in the community we call our classroom. Students are responsible for making someone feel welcome, sitting next to a variety of classmates, asking a thoughtful question, making a kind comment, solving a "puzzler" question on the chart.

In some classrooms, once Morning Meeting is familiar and established, you might also give students supervised responsibilities for specific portions of the

*Students can help with modeling
new activities.*

meeting. For example, younger children might do well with beginning a greeting or activity. Just be sure you rotate responsibilities evenly.

As students get older, the key to keeping Morning Meetings successful is for the teacher to still be the meeting planner and facilitator but to figure out ways to give class members added responsibility as they show they are ready for it. For example, later in the year when all students are comfortable with the routines of Morning Meeting, you could have students sign up to be Morning Meeting Assistants. They could help you explain or model new greetings or activities.

Older students can also help out with Morning Meeting in younger grades, perhaps going into a younger classroom once a week to help model components of the meeting.

Communicate with parents about Morning Meeting

Parents are very supportive of Morning Meeting when they understand its format and goals. But if their first impression is formed from a child's report of a "new game we played at Morning Meeting," they may draw the mistaken conclusion that this is time taken away from learning. Ongoing communication with parents will help them see Morning Meeting for the vital learning time that it is. Following are two ways you can help parents learn about Morning Meeting.

Send a letter describing Morning Meeting

A first step might be to send a letter to parents giving them a glimpse of this part of their child's day and describing the learning integral to it. You'll find a sample letter shown at right.

Invite parents to observe or participate in Morning Meeting

Often all the explanations about what students are seeing and doing in school and why they're doing it come alive and make more sense when parents experience classroom life for themselves. I've found it helpful to post a calendar on the classroom website, with three slots available on each Morning Meeting visiting day. Parents can then sign up for a time that works for them.

Make clear whether you're inviting parents to observe or actively participate in the meeting—or leaving the choice up to them. Some parents feel comfortable participating; others would rather watch first and perhaps participate at a later visit. Either way, knowing what's expected can help make their visit comfortable and productive.

An additional way for parents to observe Morning Meeting—one that might work well for parents who can't come to school during regular school hours—is to use open house time. One year my students and I did a Morning Meeting during our open house to let parents see what Morning Meeting is all about and give them a taste of the rich learning that happens in meetings every day. It was so successful that I made it a regular part of open houses from then on.

One developmental consideration: If you teach adolescents, think about whether or not they'll be comfortable having parents in the classroom. If you think that a parental visit will feel awkward or will interfere with the meeting, consider alternative ways for parents to experience Morning Meeting. For example, you could use technology to offer parents the choice of seeing Morning Meeting without being physically in the classroom.

Dear Parents,

There's a wonderful beginning to your child's school day! It's called Morning Meeting and it's a great way to build community, set a positive tone, increase excitement about learning, and improve academic and social skills.

Morning Meeting usually takes between twenty and thirty minutes. First thing each morning, the children and I gather in a circle. We begin by greeting each other. Every day, your child hears his or her name spoken by a classmate in a friendly and cheerful manner.

Next, students share interesting news with each other in a structured way. Sometimes we go around the circle and all students share; other times a few students share and have a conversation with the class. Sharing helps students listen carefully, think about what they hear, formulate good questions, and learn about each other. During sharing, children have a chance to feel that their ideas are valued and that the other children care.

After sharing, there is an activity for the whole class. We might sing or recite a poem or play a math game. The activity time helps the class feel united as a group, reinforces academic skills, and helps the children learn how to cooperate and solve problems.

Finally, we read the morning message chart, which helps students think about the day ahead. Sometimes, I use this time to review and practice a reading, punctuation, or math skill.

Every day, Morning Meeting lets children know that school is a safe place where all children's feelings and ideas are important. We'd love to have you visit a Morning Meeting. Just give me a call to arrange a good time. You'll see for yourself why we're so excited about this start to our day.

Overview

Morning Meeting responsibilities

In implementing and assessing Morning Meeting, keep the following general responsibilities in mind.

Teachers' Responsibilities

- Make sure the space is adequate and appropriate for the component. Can a circle form? Can all be seen? Can a particular game be safely played?

- Plan a meeting that supports students' academic and social-emotional learning.

- Teach Morning Meeting skills and routines one step at a time, building a scaffold so children can participate successfully in increasingly complex meetings.

- Make necessary accommodations and modifications so that all students can participate.

- Act as timekeeper, keeping things moving.

- Facilitate the meeting, making sure that all class members are greeted, that a variety of students are responding during sharing, and that everyone is participating safely and respectfully in each component.

- Observe students' skills—both social and academic.

- Notice behaviors and reinforce, remind, and redirect using positive language.

- Make sure everyone in the classroom (paraprofessionals, visitors if they wish, other adults) is included in the meeting.

Morning Meetings invite students to assume responsibility and actively participate.

┌─── **Students' Responsibilities** ───┐

- Get to the meeting promptly and form the circle safely and efficiently.

- Participate fully—contributing actively, listening well, and responding appropriately.

- Interact with a variety of classmates in the friendly spirit of Morning Meeting.

- Move smoothly from Morning Meeting to the next activity.

FINE TUNINGS

Q A couple of my students really struggle with behavior and disrupt the whole meeting. How can I help them be part of the meeting and not disrupt it?

ANSWER ▪ Students vary a great deal in their ability to follow meeting rules. The teacher's knowledge of the individual child is the starting point for any action. Is the child younger than most peers and simply not yet ready for the expectations that are appropriate for the rest of the group? Do special needs make participation particularly challenging?

For the child who is simply too young, a special arrangement about the length of time he attends Morning Meeting makes sense. Give a signal that will let him know when he is to leave the circle, and discuss what he'll do during the remaining meeting time. Gradually, as he is successful with sitting still and paying attention, extend the time he spends in the meeting.

Sometimes a bit of situational assistance is all that is needed. "Miranda, I notice that you have a hard time listening to other people when you sit next to Jin-Ping. You need to pick a different place to sit at Morning Meeting."

Or to the fidgeter whose fancy gizmo-watch treats everyone to a rendition of the "Star Wars" theme at least twice in every meeting, "Your watch needs to be in your cubby during Morning Meeting, Gerard."

Some students with lots of overflowing energy are better able to concentrate if they have something that quietly occupies their hands during Morning Meeting. But what about fairness when the rule is to come to the meeting circle empty-handed? This is a complex question about justice that repeats itself with variations all through our lives. In sorting out what to do in each circumstance, we need to consider that fair treatment is responsive to individual needs and doesn't always mean treating people with cookie-cutter sameness. When students trust that their needs, too, will be met in the same spirit of fairness, they are generally able to understand and accept modifications that you make for their classmates.

Sometimes a student's behavior is symptomatic of a need that requires more specialized intervention. A teacher in a fourth/fifth grade inclusion classroom provided a very skillful intervention for a particular student. Andrew was a fifth grader whose special needs manifested in his blurting out inappropriate and rude remarks often unconnected to anything preceding them. This was especially a problem when the class began doing dialogue sharing, in which one person at a time shares information and the rest of the class listens and responds. It became clear that Andrew needed some targeted and intensive instruction so that he could participate in this part of the meeting.

On days when the class did dialogue sharing, Andrew and one of his teachers, Ms. Scamardella (Ms. S), left the circle and moved to a table in the opposite corner of the room where Andrew had "private sharing" with Ms. S while co-teacher Ms. Daggett continued the meeting. In his private sharing, Andrew practiced sharing a piece of news appropriately, with no swearing or name-calling. Ms. S modeled careful patterns of suitable responses. Then she shared a piece of news and helped him learn to choose and practice a polite response.

After a few months, Andrew was able to rejoin the group for dialogue sharing, listening quietly most days, and on a really good day, offering a comment or a question "on the spot." In addition, the teachers carefully scheduled Andrew's times to be the sharer so that they could help him plan and rehearse what he would say.

This example illustrates an important point: Students' readiness for participation in Morning Meeting can vary widely. They may need a considerable range of modifications or support so they can participate fully in Morning Meeting. If a student is not participating, if her participation is "stuck" in the negative, or if he is spending more time in the time-out chair than in the meeting circle, then clearly the teacher must pay special attention and address the situation, calling on the support of special education staff when needed.

Overview

Q I have several children who frequently come in late and a couple who have to leave in the middle of the meeting for special programs. Should they be part of Morning Meeting?

ANSWER ▪ Yes, definitely. Morning Meeting is for everyone. Frustrating as the tardiness may be, the meeting time itself is not the time to address it. Latecomers should be greeted pleasantly and welcomed without unduly disrupting whatever is happening in the meeting. To minimize the disruption while still making the latecomer feel welcome, some teachers assign a child the daily job of welcoming latecomers into the circle.

If the lateness is occasional, simply help the child fit into the flow of the day. If it is a chronic problem with a particular child, then some investigation and problem-solving is in order.

In the case of students who have to leave early for "specials," make sure that the greeting can happen with them in the circle and teach them how to leave the circle quietly and unobtrusively when it is time. If the same students must leave every day, you might think about scheduling a separate time for sharing near the end of the day when everyone can attend.

Q My students are really comfortable with our Morning Meeting, maybe too comfortable. Even I sometimes feel like it's boring. Help!

ANSWER ▪ A sensitive balance exists between the lovely sense of security that routine can provide and the monotony that can creep in when that routine is unchanging. As students grow comfortable with each other and with the basic format of Morning Meeting, the teacher must act as the "re-balancer" and introduce variation.

This is one reason why retaining the role of meeting planner is so important for teachers even if they shift some of the meeting responsibilities to students as the year unfolds. Just as in an academic lesson, we need to plan a meeting that will keep students engaged. How can we vary the content and format of each component? How can students interact around meaningful content that is connected to both their interests and the curriculum? Is the content in the meeting too easy or too hard? How much active learning is involved? Are students sitting too long or are they up and moving during different parts of the meeting?

I find that when teachers consistently consider these questions, purposeful and engaging Morning Meetings result. But if teachers frequently run meetings "on the fly," the meetings can quickly become boring and stale.

Q **Students in my classroom usually choose to sit next to their friends. Any ideas for making this work better?**

A N S W E R ▪ Calling this seating habit to students' attention, within the context of the larger purposes of Morning Meeting, is often enough intervention. "I notice," says the teacher, "that for the last several mornings, many of us have been choosing to sit next to our good friends. Remember that one of the purposes of Morning Meeting is to help us get to know and feel comfortable with everyone—including those who are not already our friends. Think about that when you choose where you will sit this morning." Tying what may seem a superficial detail to our grander vision helps students see the underlying significance of where we choose to sit and why this choice merits attention.

Sometimes formalizing these expectations and then using verbal cues is necessary. "Boys next to girls" and "new friends' day" can be useful shorthand for reminding students of expectations. In a fifth/sixth grade classroom, the teacher noticed that students were clustering by gender and clique in a raggedy circle. "Meeting seating," he said, reminding students of expectations and structures established early in the school year. Students quickly reassembled into an even circle, with an alternating boy-girl pattern.

Teachers can also engineer different mixes that shake up entrenched patterns. In some primary classes, students make and decorate "sit-upons" with their names.

Teachers then use these cushions to assign seats, rotating placement often so that children sit next to many class members. In older classes, a round of A Warm Wind Blows, the Skip Greeting, or the Baseball Greeting (pages 156, 81, and 72) will shake up the seating arrangement.

Sometimes students themselves will notice a problem—and will have great ideas for addressing it. One winter morning when I called the fourth grade students to Morning Meeting, a student raised his hand. "Mrs. Davis," he said, "everyone always sits next to the same person each day in Morning Meeting." Around the circle, his classmates nodded in agreement. Later that day during our closing circle, we decided to create a list of patterns we could use to arrange ourselves in Morning Meeting. It was an extremely long list including ideas such as ABC order according to first, middle, or last name; boy/girl; numerical order according to their house or apartment number; birthday order; alternating color of eyes (blue, brown, green); sit next to a new person every day; sit next to someone from a different table; and so on. I was amazed by what the group came up with.

We decided to post a different seating order each day on our morning message to guide how students arranged themselves in the circle. However, I made sure that a couple of days each week were free-choice seating days, because the ultimate goal was to have them choose to meet and interact with a variety of people.

Q **In my classroom, there is a child nobody wants to sit next to. How should I address this?**

ANSWER ▪ Frequently students deliberately ostracize a certain child by not sitting next to him or her. Action is required on two fronts—one immediate, the other longer term.

First, do whatever you must to stop the exclusion-by-seating. Remove the element of choice by assigning rotating seating patterns (see previous question). Or assign partners who will sit together at Morning Meeting and work together during any partner activities within the meeting.

The longer-term solution begins with observing and reflecting on why this child is not accepted. Is this an instance of bullying or pre-bullying behavior? Or is some other dynamic at play? Is a specific group of students doing the excluding? Or is this a whole-class problem?

If specific children seem to lead the exclusionary actions, you could set up a time to talk with them, both to understand more about what's going on and to make clear that this is not acceptable behavior. If it's a whole-class problem, you could schedule a class discussion, at a separate time from Morning Meeting. However, you'll need to carefully structure the discussion in a way that protects the child who has been ostracized. One way to do this is to read and discuss a book chosen for its relevant plot, which allows the discussion of the social issue to happen at a slight remove from actual classroom circumstances.

Q What is the difference between a class meeting and Morning Meeting?

ANSWER ▪ Class meetings are held for the purpose of solving a problem, or perhaps planning for a project or event or debriefing afterwards. They are generally not held every day.

Morning Meetings are held for the purposes named earlier and are held every day. They are not used as a time to solve problems or take care of general classroom business. Teachers who use both kinds of meetings often comment that many of the habits of participation and social skills that are developed through Morning Meeting help students succeed with democratic, cooperative processes like class meetings.

*Many teachers create a standard Morning Meeting plan that
guest teachers can use when the classroom teacher is absent.*

Q **I have students in my class from diverse cultural backgrounds,
many of whom are learning to speak English. Are there special
things I should keep in mind when planning Morning Meetings?**

ANSWER ▪ When you think about how to adapt Morning Meeting for use with
English language learners, it's important to spend some time learning about the
students' countries of origin so you can understand the particular challenges each
child might face and the strengths each might bring. Although it's best to learn
from the students and their families, some time spent in the library or on the
Internet is also worthwhile. Here are some questions to ask:

- What are the traditions for greeting people in the student's culture?

- What has the student probably learned about how to behave toward adults?
  Toward peers? Toward peers of the same gender? Of a different gender?

- Is it culturally acceptable to touch a classmate? Is it culturally acceptable
  to make eye contact?

- What are the expectations regarding education for boys? For girls?

Knowing the answers to some of these questions will help you plan Morning Meeting structures that will ease the student's transition. For example, if a child is not accustomed to touching other people, a greeting in which children pass a ball or other small object around the circle (see page 71) can help him begin to feel comfortable with physically interactive greetings. And if you have taken the time to learn about family and cultural customs, you may be able to invite the student to share them through Morning Meeting—for example, by having the class do a greeting using a common greeting phrase from her home culture. This helps her feel welcomed while enriching the class's learning and appreciation of world cultures.

Overview

Q Morning Meeting runs well when I'm in the classroom, but I'm concerned what will happen when I'm out and a guest teacher is there. How can I ensure success for both the guest teacher and the students?

ANSWER ▪ With some planning on your part, guest teachers can be very successful with Morning Meeting. First, create a standard Morning Meeting plan that can be used when you're absent. Keep it simple but engaging for children. In your notes to the guest teacher, explain the four components and write out directions for each. For the morning message, one idea that has worked well for me is to write a standard message on a chart and laminate it so that each time you have a guest teacher, you or the guest teacher can put in the correct date and other customizations with dry erase markers.

Next, practice this standard Morning Meeting with students prior to having a guest teacher. Be sure students know how to do each of the components, and address any possible snags. I sometimes have invited a colleague to take the role of guest teacher while I was there so I could observe, see where the rough spots might be, and make adjustments.

Greeting

**A FRIENDLY AND
RESPECTFUL SALUTE**

"Good morning, Morgan." Hector speaks seriously and earnestly, for that is who Hector is. He looks directly at Morgan, who sits on his left, and offers his right hand.

"Good morning, Hector!" returns Morgan. He grins widely and grasps Hector's hand with exuberance. Morgan's "Good mornings" are always punctuated with invisible exclamation points, for that is who Morgan is.

Shannon, on Morgan's left, shifts a bit and sits up taller, ready to receive the enthusiasm of a greeting, Morgan-style. And here it comes. "Good morning, Shannon!" "Good morning, Morgan!" Her teacher smiles, pleased with Shannon's strong voice. Shannon had entered the third grade classroom in September with a tentative air. In Morning Meetings, her fade-into-the-chair posture and barely audible voice seemed designed to help her escape the notice of her peers. Now, four months and more than seventy Morning Meetings later, here she is, wearing a smile almost as broad as Morgan's, her hand extended and waiting for his.

And so it goes around the circle. Greeting takes slightly less than three minutes. Every member of the circle—children, teacher, assistant teacher, and Matthew's mother, who is visiting this morning—has been greeted by name, with a handshake and a friendly smile.

PURPOSES AND REFLECTIONS

Morning Meetings begin with greeting. Even on days when time doesn't allow for a full Morning Meeting, teachers convene the circle and make sure greeting takes place. It is that important because of the tone it sets and the way that tone carries into the rest of the day.

Some mornings, the greeting is basic and straightforward, as described in the opening vignette. Variations might be simple, such as students tossing a ball to the person whom they are greeting or substituting a high five for the handshake. Other mornings, the greeting process is more elaborate. Some greetings work with all ages; others have features that make them appropriate only for younger grades or complex steps better suited to older students.

Although the primary purposes of greeting are interpersonal, greetings also offer an opportunity to practice academic skills. For example, in Skip Greeting (page 81), students practice counting or learning about intervals; in Adjective Greeting (page 70), students practice their knowledge of descriptive words. However, we take care to keep the skills being practiced simple and familiar enough that the focus remains on the greeting itself.

Long or short, dignified or playful, greetings share four common purposes that are explored in the following sections.

Purposes of Greeting

- Sets a positive tone for the classroom and the day
- Provides a sense of recognition and belonging
- Helps students learn and use each other's names
- Gives practice in offering hospitality

Greeting can be simple and straightforward.
Here, first graders pass a simple greeting around the circle.

Greeting sets a positive tone for the classroom and the day

Welcoming, friendly, respectful—these are attributes that characterize the climate in exemplary classrooms. Beginning Morning Meeting with greeting helps create such a climate.

Having a designated greeting each day is important. Though greeting allows plenty of room for individual personality to shine through—Hector's "Good morning" is different from Morgan's, which is different from Shannon's—it also has a structure that provides equity and safety.

The goal in Morning Meeting greeting is for all to greet and be greeted equally. Within a classroom community, starting a day by hearing your name spoken with respect and warmth is not a privilege for just a popular few. It is, instead, a right to which all are entitled. When we make time for greeting every morning, no matter how full the schedule, we make a statement as teachers that we expect class members to treat each other with courtesy and equity and that we will do our best to make sure that they do so.

Being greeted provides a sense of recognition and belonging

Being greeted by name is a very basic way of gaining a sense of recognition and belonging. In *The Fifth Discipline Fieldbook* (Senge, 1994, p. 3), Peter Senge tells of the most common greeting among the tribes of Natal in South Africa. The greeting in Zulu, *Sawubona*, translates literally as "I see you." The standard reply is *Sikhona*, "I am here." The order of these phrases is important: One cannot be present until one is seen. The truth of this perception extends beyond linguistic convention.

My student Sue (whom you met in the Introduction) went ungreeted and unseen for seven-eighths of her day. Unseen, she felt she was not there. Because she was old enough to do something about it, she chose to physically remove herself. Sadly, our classrooms have too many other children who, though physically present, walk through their days feeling unacknowledged and unseen.

I think of the old expression "neither here nor there," meaning something that is unimportant and irrelevant, the opposite of how we want our students to feel.

These fifth graders practice the skills of respectful greeting: looking at each other, touching hands gently, saying the person's name clearly.

We want them to feel important, to be "here." And so they must feel seen. The act of intentional greeting is an act of sincere recognition of each child, every day.

Making sure that everyone sees and is seen is especially important in upper grades. Developmentally, upper grade children are figuring out how to form intense, loyal affiliations. One way they do this is by forming cliques or other tightly bonded and highly exclusive groups.

It's particularly important for this age group to learn how to welcome everyone and form groups with people other than their closest friends. Looking each other in the eye, smiling, and greeting each other by name—or a self-chosen nickname—is an important and powerful demonstration of respect that is witnessed by the entire group.

Greeting helps students learn and use each other's names

Knowing someone's name and feeling comfortable using it provides many options for personal connection. It lets us call on each other during a discussion. It is a way we get each other's attention, enabling us to ask a question, request help, offer congratulations, or whisper an apology.

We can't assume that just because students are grouped together they will all learn each other's names. Halfway through the school year, a math teacher from a small regional school, where students from several adjacent towns met for the first time in seventh grade, asked a student to hand a set of papers back to the class. He was surprised to find that she couldn't do it. Why? She couldn't match the names on the papers with the faces of her peers. She simply didn't know all her classmates' names.

A student who doesn't know her classmates well enough to hand them their work is unlikely to feel familiar enough with them to offer her dissenting opinion about a character in a short story, or admit that she doesn't quite get this business of "3 is to 21 as x is to 28," or share a poem she wrote about her grandmother. And what a loss that would be, both for her and for her classmates.

Knowing that others know our name and hearing our name used is also a reminder of our identity, our individuality within a larger whole. Students identify with their school, their class within that school, their athletic teams, and other extracurricular groups they may be part of. They are Pine Street School students, Bluefish swimmers, or Girl Scout Troop #33. While we value feeling a part of larger communities, it's also essential to retain our sense of individuality. Hearing our name lets us know that someone cares about speaking to us as an individual. Our name allows us to claim ownership when we are proud of what we have created, a stamp that lets the world know we exist and that what we have done is important.

Greeting provides practice in offering hospitality

Educator and author Parker Palmer writes, "Hospitality is always an act that benefits the host even more than the guest. The concept of hospitality arose in ancient times when this reciprocity was easier to see: In nomadic cultures, the food and shelter one gave to a stranger yesterday is the food and shelter one hopes to receive from a stranger tomorrow. By offering hospitality, one participates in the endless reweaving of a social fabric on which all can depend" (Palmer, 1998, p. 50).

Welcoming each other to our classroom every day is an act of hospitality. The offering of that welcome, one to another, affirms that we are caretakers of each other in that community. Being a host also implies, builds, and strengthens a person's ownership and investment in that place.

We practice daily the skills of welcoming each other—the clear voice, the friendly smile, the careful remembering that Nicholas likes to be called Nick, the firm handshake. When guests visit and are part of our circle, we extend a welcome to them as well, although it can feel a bit awkward at first. "Should we call him Mike or Mr. DiAngelo?" whispers Andy to his teacher when he notices that his friend Matt's father is coming to Morning Meeting. "Could you check with him and see which would feel more comfortable?" replies his teacher.

Several important messages are conveyed in this suggestion. First, our culture offers no single right answer to the question of how to address elders. Some parents prefer being called by their first names; others deem it disrespectful. Second, the role of a host is to make the guest feel respected and comfortable. And third, asking a polite and direct question is a fine way to get an answer you need. It is practice in assertiveness seasoned with courtesy, not an easy blend to achieve at any age.

Kindergarten teacher Eileen Mariani related the story of a January morning in her room.

> The habit of greeting within the Morning Meeting circle had been well established. On that particular morning it was Isaac's turn to begin the greeting. Isaac was a shy boy who approached this task with some trepidation. Eileen watched carefully, ready to help if Isaac seemed worried at any point. But, no need, he was doing splendidly.

Greeting

> "Good Morning, Friends" (page 75) was the greeting and it had been clapped and stamped with a nicely modulated glee around the circle, just returning to Isaac, when he glanced up and then stood abruptly, heading for the door. Eileen, whose view of the door was blocked by a bookshelf, also rose to see what was going on. There stood Isaac, framed by the doorway, hand extended to a distinguished-looking visitor who was entering the room with the principal. "Good morning, Mr. . . . uh . . . I'm sorry, what is your name, please?" Isaac proceeded to shake the visitor's hand before walking gravely back to his place on the rug to continue the meeting.

The months of modeling and practicing, the discussions of "What can you do if you don't remember someone's name?" had taken hold and enabled Isaac to extend graceful hospitality and true welcome, not just during Morning Meeting with classmates, but beyond it, even to a stranger at the door.

Highlights of Greeting

- Ensures that every child names and notices others at the outset of the day and is named in return

- Allows the teacher to observe and "take the pulse" of the group that day

- Provides practice in elements of effective communication, such as looking at each other, using a friendly voice and friendly body language, speaking clearly and audibly, listening respectfully, and waiting one's turn

- Requires students to extend the range of classmates they spontaneously notice and greet

- Helps students to reach across gender, clique, and friendship lines

- Challenges the intellect (when the greeting structure uses math patterns, phrases in various languages, and set making, for example) and provides practice in academic skills
---

Before continuing on to the next section, you may want to browse through "Greetings to Try" starting on page 68 to get a sense of the wide range of possible greetings.

GETTING STARTED

Pay attention to the words you use to introduce greeting

"Every morning, we're going to greet each other in a friendly and respectful way," a seventh grade teacher says as she introduces greeting to students. With this simple sentence she has noted and named two elements of successful greetings. She doesn't stop there—she follows up with discussion, modeling, and practice to make sure that students understand what a friendly and respectful greeting looks and sounds like. But those first words used to introduce greeting establish basic expectations from the outset.

Setting an expectation of friendliness and respect is especially important with upper grade students, whose friendships can be intense and exclusive. With older children, I clarify that I don't expect them to be best friends with everyone in the class, but I do expect them to be friendly and to treat everyone with respect. We then take time to discuss the details. What does it sound like to say "Good morning" with a friendly tone? What does a firm handshake feel like? Paying attention to these details makes a tremendous difference in the success of greeting.

Model and practice greeting routines and procedures

Even in the most basic "Good morning" greeting, students need to look at their classmate, and, using the classmate's name, say "Good morning" with a friendly tone and a clear voice. That's a lot to remember.

For greeting to go smoothly and be a positive start to the day, it's important to model and practice common skills. These include:

- Sitting or standing in your own space in the circle
- Speaking in a clear, audible voice
- Using a friendly tone
- Using friendly body language
- Shaking hands safely
- Waiting your turn
- Listening while others greet

Interactive Modeling, as described on pages 26–27, is a good strategy to use for teaching greeting skills. You might begin the modeling by saying, "Our rules say 'Be kind to each other.' One way to do that is to be sure we greet each other in a friendly way. Watch while I greet John and notice what I do that is friendly."

When you ask the class what they noticed during the demonstration, guide them in naming all the important elements: looking at the person being greeted, smiling, using his or her name, and using a friendly voice.

In the days that follow, and periodically throughout the year, reinforce these and any additional greeting skills the class learns. For example, "What did you notice about the way we did our greeting today?" "What makes it easier to speak loudly and clearly?"

Keep greetings simple at first

When first introducing greeting, a simple, direct "Good morning, [classmate's name]" works best. When students are able to do that fluently and in a consistently friendly way, introduce other elements, keeping in mind students' ages, skill levels, and experience with Morning Meeting.

Here is one possible progression (be sure to model each element you add):

- Teach a basic "Good morning" greeting (page 76)
- Add an item such as a ball or soft toy for students to pass around the circle
- Add a handshake or other physical contact
- Add movement, music, or both
- Add an element of choice (choosing a movement to make, choosing a classmate to greet)

Help students learn each other's names

Name tags are a great help in the early days of school, and many greetings focus on learning names (pages 68–83). With young children, starting the year with chorus greetings, in which everyone says or sings the names together, can help the children feel more comfortable in the process of learning classmates' names. When the children are ready to say names individually, assigning pairs ahead of time so that each person is prepared to say a partner's name can help boost children's confidence.

Older children also benefit from structures that help them learn names. On the first day of school, I often issue a challenge: "Let's see if all of us can learn each other's names by the end of the second week of school." Students eagerly take up

Once students have the basic greeting skills down, you can teach some more elaborate greetings. Here, kindergartners pass around a fanciful handshake.

the challenge and many of them feel confident that they'll learn names in the first week. At the end of the challenge period, I give students a chance to see if they can name everyone in the meeting circle. I love seeing the smiles as students hear their name.

Use opportunities to practice academic skills

In addition to building community and helping students feel welcomed, greeting can be a time for reviewing academic content or practicing academic skills.

For example, a Skip Greeting (page 81), which can be adapted for any age group, offers an opportunity to practice math skills. Younger children get to practice counting; older children can take responsibility for calculating the number of "skips" needed to ensure that all are greeted. Or if the class is learning about adjectives, students can each greet their neighbor and add "I'm having a _____ day so far. What about you?" with each student filling in the blank with an adjective.

In Greetings to Try (beginning on page 68) you'll find a number of greetings that incorporate academic content or skills practice.

Consider ways for students to take responsibility for aspects of greeting

Although you, as teacher, will want to keep hold of planning and managing Morning Meeting, you can give students responsibility for aspects of greeting. For example, you might give individuals responsibility for choosing the day's greeting from a short list of familiar greetings (be sure to rotate this privilege among all students; also check on their choice ahead of time to make sure it fits the needs of the group on that day).

Another way to give students responsibility, especially later in the year, is to have them devise new greetings. One year, when I was teaching fourth grade, students collaborated in language arts block to create and write up ideas for new greetings. I worked with them to refine their ideas and then incorporated these greetings into our Morning Meetings, asking the students to help me introduce and model each one.

Anticipate and help students handle awkward moments

Norah turns to greet Shane but in the moment forgets his name. Or as a class nears the end of a Ball Toss greeting (page 71), Josiah freezes and then tosses the ball to a student who has already been greeted. Awkward moments happen. Although it's not possible to avoid all such moments, anticipation and planning can diminish their frequency and intensity.

Sometimes the solution is as simple as posing a question before the greeting: "What can we do if we forget someone's name?" During the brief discussion that follows, students conclude that they can nicely ask someone's name. They also suggest that if they see the person greeting them hesitate, they can help out by whispering their name. For greetings that require students to notice and remember who has been greeted, teachers might devise a signal ("thumbs up until you're greeted"). Such signals help the last few greeters who may be struggling to remember who remains to be greeted.

As greetings get more complex or higher in risk, you'll need to anticipate potentially hurtful situations. Sometimes students get into a pattern of greeting the most popular classmates first and leaving the same students, over and over, to be greeted last. If you notice this dynamic occurring, remind students that the purpose of greeting is for all to feel welcomed and part of the group. Then select greetings that encourage students to move out of their friendship groups. For example, you might do a Cross-Circle Greeting (page 73) and ask students to greet someone across the circle to whom they haven't spoken that morning.

Greeting responsibilities

In implementing and assessing greeting, keep the following general responsibilities in mind.

──── **Teachers' Responsibilities** ────

- Teach a variety of age-appropriate greetings.

- Model aspects of a warm and respectful greeting.

- Make sure everyone uses friendly and appropriate words and body language.

- As students are ready, give them responsibility for choosing greetings.

- Teach greeting skills and routines gradually, building a scaffold so students can participate successfully in increasingly complex greetings.

──── **Students' Responsibilities** ────

- Vary whom they sit next to.

- Wait for their turn to greet.

- Listen carefully to the other greetings.

- Use a clear, audible voice.

- Use friendly and appropriate body language and tone of voice.

FINE TUNINGS

Q Do I need to do greeting every single day? What about days when we have no time, when the art teacher is waiting to start the art lesson or we're going on a field trip and need to leave right away?

ANSWER ▪ It's important to do greeting every day, but greeting doesn't need to take a lot of time. When time is tight you could do a greeting like Righty-Lefty (page 80), in which students turn and greet their neighbors all at the same time.

For the "Tuesday-is-art-right-away" situation, where the time crunch will be regular, you might suggest that the art teacher join you for five minutes to be part of the class greeting before beginning the art lesson.

On field trip days, teachers sometimes gather students after reaching their destination for a brief check-in and a simple greeting.

Q How might I need to adapt greeting so that it supports ELL students?

ANSWER ▪ Simple greetings that require only a word—or no words at all—are a good starting point for ELL students. For students just learning English, begin with just a wave and a smile. Then add simple words such as "Hi," "Hello," "Good morning," followed by learning the pronunciation of classmates' names. Continue to add more complex language as students are ready. Giving students a chance to practice the greetings with a partner or small group before using them in Morning Meeting can also be helpful.

Additionally, songs and chants are wonderful ways for ELL students to become comfortable with new language forms. Often, phrases that are hard to say fluently are much easier when set to music.

Keep in mind that every culture has its own way of greeting people, and that students from some cultures might feel a tension between classroom greetings and what they are accustomed to. For example, some students have been taught at home to avoid eye contact with each other or, more often, with adults as an indication of respect. In some countries, hugging or shaking hands is a gesture of friendship. In other countries, it's not culturally acceptable to touch other people. In yet other countries, cross-gender handshakes are taboo, whereas same-gender friends greet each other with a kiss. This is where it pays to do a little research into students' home cultures.

Greetings that use a prop such as a ball or soft toy (page 71) can bridge the gap between cultures. Looking at someone is easier when you must be sure that your classmate is ready before you toss the ball. And ball-pass greetings can help children begin to feel comfortable with physically interactive greetings.

Another idea is to have all students learn to greet each other in the home languages of the ELL students. The ELL students may feel more welcomed and the native English speakers would have an opportunity to gain some insight into the difficulties of functioning in a new language.

Q **What about the child who just doesn't speak in front of the group? How can I help him participate in greeting?**

ANSWER ▪ This is not uncommon. Children might refrain from speaking in the meeting due to shyness or difficulty with English or as a manifestation of special needs. As the question implies, finding a way to make sure that these children are part of the routine is important.

Something that often helps is practicing with the child individually before the meeting and making sure that he knows whom he will greet. Kindergarten teacher Elisabeth Olivera, who teaches in a bilingual classroom, suggests that the teacher and student say the words together, with the teacher gradually softening her voice until the child is comfortable speaking on his own. I have provided this sort of support to older students as well.

You can also help the group understand what is going on and how they can be encouraging. The explanation should be simple and matter-of-fact. For the young and reluctant speaker, you might say, "Terry doesn't want to talk in Morning Meeting yet, but I hope that he will soon. Until he does, you can help by making sure he is greeted, and I will help by greeting the next person with him."

This is a wonderful opportunity to validate that we all have different comfort levels with different activities, and that we can help one another by being accepting and encouraging.

Q Students seem to be getting bored with greeting. What can I do?

ANSWER ▪ First, think about the source of the boredom. Is it time to add variety? Or has the class turned a developmental corner? Perhaps greetings that were safe and right for mostly sevens, for example, are feeling too narrow for eight-year-olds, who crave some sanctioned ways to vent their boisterous side.

To add variety, take a look at the week as a whole and then find ways to vary the greetings day to day. For example, one day pass a greeting around the circle, another day do a group chant as a greeting, and another day do a greeting that involves movement or one where students get to choose whom to greet.

Besides introducing new greetings, you can work with students to come up with adaptations of old favorites. For example, a group of fifth graders at Kensington Avenue Elementary School in Springfield, Massachusetts, invented the Elbow Rock Greeting (page 75) in which they extend arms, bent at the elbow, and shake arms rather than hands.

Q I teach in the upper grades and students usually start out fine with greeting. However, as the year goes on, they tend to get sloppy and silly. They complain that greeting is babyish and that they know everyone's names and don't see why they have to keep doing this.

ANSWER ▪ This is not an unusual occurrence, particularly with older students as they get used to Morning Meeting, comfortable with the class, and lax with expectations. When you see behaviors such as whispering, nudging, in-jokes, fake smiles, and muttered names, it's time to stop the meeting. These kinds of behaviors are a signal that the class has lost sight of the real purpose behind greeting and needs some help to get back on track.

Greeting

Review the goals and purposes of greeting. Remind the group that greetings welcome and acknowledge people in the classroom community and that this is important work. Sometimes sharing a story with the students, such as the one offered earlier about Sue (who never felt acknowledged) or the story of a time when you, as an adult, felt unnoticed, helps to remind children of the importance of what they are doing. A discussion about how a sincere versus an insincere greeting really feels may also be helpful. You might ask the students for suggestions of ways to make greeting work better while also holding them to the expectation that they greet each other in a respectful and friendly way.

GREETINGS TO TRY

Greeting	Beginning of Year	Later in Year	Younger Grades	Older Grades	Song, Chant, Movement	Academic Content Reinforcement
Adjective, p. 70		●	●	●		●
Albert Einstein, p. 70	●			●	●	●
Ball Toss, p. 71	●		●	●		
Ball Toss Variations for Upper Grades, p. 71	●			●		
Baseball, p. 72		●	●	●		
Book Character, p. 72		●	●	●		●
Cheer, p. 72		●		●	●	
Cross-Circle, p. 73	●		●	●		
Dice, p. 73		●		●		●
Different Languages, p. 74	●		●	●		●
Double-Takes, p. 74		●		●		
Elbow Rock, p. 75		●		●		
"Good Morning, Friends," p. 75		●	●		●	
"Good Morning," p. 76	●	●	●	●		
"Good Morning" Using Props, p. 77	●		●	●		●
"Hello, Neighbor," p. 77		●	●		●	

Greeting	Beginning of Year	Later in Year	Younger Grades	Older Grades	Song, Chant, Movement	Academic Content Reinforcement
Interview, p. 78	●		●	●		
Knock, Knock, p. 78	●		●			
Marbles, p. 78		●	●	●		
Math Match Card, p. 79	●			●	●	●
Name Card, p. 79	●		●	●		
One-Minute, p. 79		●	●	●		
One, Two, Three, Four, p. 80		●		●	●	
Pantomime, p. 80	●		●	●		
Righty/Lefty, p. 80		●	●	●		
Sawubona–Sikhona, p. 81		●		●		
Science Friction, p. 81	●		●		●	●
Skip, p. 81		●		●		●
Snowball, p. 82		●	●	●		
Spider Web, p. 82		●	●	●		
What's Your Place Value?, p. 83		●	●	●		●

Greetings to Try

Adjective Greeting

Each student chooses an adjective that begins with the same sound as his or her first name. Going around the circle, students introduce themselves by saying, "Hello, my name is [adjective] [first name]." For example, "Hello, my name is Jazzy Janet!" Classmates respond, "Hello, Jazzy Janet!"

Before starting the greeting, take a few minutes for the group to brainstorm a list of adjectives that you write on the board or chart. Guide students toward positive words. Add adjectives as needed to ensure that several adjectives begin with the initial letter or sound of each student's name.

VARIATION ▪ If there's time, students often like the challenge of going around the circle a second time and trying to name each classmate, using the classmate's chosen adjective.

Albert Einstein Greeting

In advance, find quotations by Albert Einstein (or other famous scientists) to inspire students or relate to their science learning, for example, "The important thing is to not stop questioning; curiosity has its own reason for existing." Give each student a slip of paper or index card with a different quotation on it. Then have students mix and mingle to greet each other and take turns reading their quotation and briefly sharing what it means to them. Have students greet as many classmates as time permits.

Ball Toss Greeting

A child begins by greeting another child and then gently throwing, rolling, or bouncing a ball to him. The second child returns the greeting (but not the ball). He then chooses a new classmate to greet and pass the ball to. Continue in this way until all have been greeted once. The greeting ends when the ball returns to the starter. If you're using a small, soft ball, throwing underhand works best. Roll or softly bounce a large, bouncy ball.

Ball Toss Variations for Upper Grades

Here are some variations that make the Ball Toss Greeting more challenging and more effective for building cooperation among older students.

- Pass the greeting ball around the circle as explained above. Now the ball goes around one more time silently (with no greeting or talking), repeating the pattern it just made. Students will enjoy passing the ball several times this way and competing against the clock.
- Pass the greeting ball as explained above. Repeat, passing the ball silently in the same pattern, and as the ball goes around add one or two more balls at even intervals so that several balls are being passed in the original greeting pattern. Challenge students to see if they can pass the balls around three times without dropping them or skipping anyone. You can also add the element of competition against the clock.
- Once the greeting ball has gone around the first time, have students "undo the greeting pattern" by sending it in the reverse direction while saying "Have a good day!" or some other encouraging words.

Baseball Greeting

Explain and post the following definitions: single = one base; double = two bases; triple = three bases; home run = four bases. All students stand; choose one to be the first batter. She decides what type of hit she's made (for example, a triple) and begins to walk around the inside of the circle. Each student she passes represents a base. As she passes first base and second base, she high-fives these students.

When she reaches third base, she says "Good morning, _____" to the student there. He returns her greeting, and she takes his place in the circle. She crosses her arms, the agreed-on gesture that indicates she's been greeted. He becomes the next batter and the process continues, skipping anyone who's already been greeted, until everyone has been greeted.

Book Character Greeting

For a week, students wear name tags of their favorite book character. Greetings that week can be done using characters' names. At the end of the week, have students remove their name tags and see if they can remember one another's character names.

Cheer Greeting

Going around the circle, students do the following call and response greeting:

Student: My name is [first name].
 Group: YEAH!
Student: And I like to [activity].
 Group: Uh-huh.
Student: And I'll be a [person who does this activity].
 Group: YEAH!
Student: Every day of my life.
 Group: Every day of [his/her] life.

FOR EXAMPLE:

Student: My name is Carla.
  Group: YEAH!
Student: And I like to swim.
  Group: Uh-huh.
Student: And I'll be a swimmer.
  Group: YEAH!
Student: Every day of my life.
  Group: Every day of her life.

Cross-Circle Greeting

Greetings
to Try

One-by-one, students greet someone sitting on the other side of the circle who hasn't yet been greeted. Many variations on this greeting are possible, such as cross-circle someone-wearing-the-same-color-as-you greeting, cross-circle some-one-you-haven't-spoken-to-yet-this-morning greeting, and so on. Before the greeting, agree on a signal that indicates "I've been greeted!" (crossed arms, thumbs up).

Dice Greeting

Students sit in the circle. The first student rolls a pair of dice and says a math fact about the numbers rolled. For example, if she rolls a six and a five, she could say, "Good morning! Six times five equals thirty." The rest of the class returns the greeting and repeats the math fact. The first greeter now hands the dice to the person on her left and the greeting continues around the circle.

VARIATION ▪ Challenge students not to repeat any facts. If they get stuck, let them roll the dice again to get a different combination.

Different Languages for Greeting

Students greet each other in a language other than English. The use of different languages for greeting can be incorporated into many greeting structures.

Some options include:

- American Sign Language (signing "hello" is similar to saluting: With the fingers squeezed together and the palm facing outward, touch the tips of the fingers to the forehead and then move the hand slightly forward and then sharply down)
- Marhaba (Arabic)
- Bonjou (Haitian Creole)
- Bonjour (French)
- Buenos días (Spanish)
- Buon giorno (Italian)
- Dobroe utro (Russian)
- Guten Morgen (German)
- Jambo (Swahili)
- Dzień dobry (Polish)
- Kalimera (Greek)
- Namaste (Hindi)
- Zao an (Mandarin Chinese)
- Ohayō (Japanese)
- Shalom (Hebrew)
- Xin chao (Vietnamese)

Double-Takes Greeting

Students mix and mingle to music, greeting each other with a friendly hand-shake and a "Good morning, [classmate's name]." When the music stops, students who are greeting each other form pairs and find one thing they have in common—their "double-take." After thirty seconds to a minute, invite a few pairs to share their double-takes with the class. Repeat as time allows, being sure to have different students share out each time.

Before the greeting begins, discuss with students the importance of greeting different people, not just their best friends, and guide them in thinking of strategies for helping each other do this. Also, help them think about the kinds of things they might have in common (hobbies, favorite music or TV shows, sports, etc.). If you think it might be difficult for students to find common interests, you could make the task more specific; for example, ask them to share one thing they each enjoyed about a recent field trip or a favorite song from the school band performance.

Elbow Rock Greeting

The greeting goes around the circle with each student saying "Good morning" to the next, but instead of shaking hands, the students lock elbows and shake arms.

Before the greeting, model and practice doing an "elbow shake."

"Good Morning, Friends" Greeting

The following chant is a good way to begin the greeting portion of Morning Meeting, but it should not serve as the only greeting. After the class completes the chant, they can pass around the room a simple greeting that uses each student's name.

Chant:

Good morning, friends.
Two words so nice to say.
So clap your hands,
And stamp your feet,
And let's start together this way.

"Good Morning" Greeting

In this basic greeting, two students face each other, smile, and say, "Good morning, [classmate's name]."

To vary the greeting early in the year, try having students greet each other with:

- A wave
- A salute
- A bow
- A thumbs-up
- A peace sign

After a few weeks, when students are more comfortable with each other and with the format of Morning Meeting, you might have students greet each other with:

- A handshake
- A handshake that students make up
- A high five
- A high five and ankle shake
- A pinky shake
- A touch on the shoulder
- An elbow shake

"Good Morning" Greeting Using Props

Going around the circle, students pass a prop that's associated with an academic subject and greet each other using an appropriate title. For example, students might pass a magnifying glass and say, "Good morning, scientist [classmate's name]," or pass a book and say "Good morning, reader [classmate's name]." Choose props that reinforce an academic focus for the day.

"Hello, Neighbor" Greeting

Students form an inner and an outer circle, with the inner circle facing the outer circle. Students who are facing each other are now partners who greet each other with the following chant:

Greetings
to Try

> Hello, neighbor, what d'ya say? (Wave to your partner.)
>
> It's gonna be a wonderful day. (Circle arms over head and then move down to the sides.)
>
> So clap your hands and boogie on down. (Clap hands and wiggle down.)
>
> Give a little bump and turn around. (Gently bump hips and turn in place.)

The inner circle then moves one person to the right so that everyone has a new partner and repeats the chant. This continues until everyone is back in their original places.

VARIATION ▪ Instead of bumping hips, students can jump ("Give a little jump and turn around") or raise hands high ("Then raise your hands and turn around").

Interview Greeting

On the morning message, ask students to pair up and interview each other. Provide a structure for this interview. For example, you could give students fill-in-the-blank sentences to complete or list two or three questions they can ask. During the meeting, partners introduce each other to the group: "Hi, this is [partner's name]. After school he likes to go rollerblading, and his favorite food is ice cream."

Knock, Knock Greeting

Use this variation of an old favorite to have children greet each other and learn last names. The first greeter turns to the student on her left (the receiver), smiles, and pretends to knock on a door:

>   Greeter: Knock, knock!
>   Receiver: Who's there?
>   Greeter: Maya.
>   Receiver: Maya who?
>   Greeter: Maya Gonzalez!
>   Receiver and group chant: Good morning, Maya Gonzalez!

The receiver becomes the next greeter. Go around the circle until everyone has been greeted.

Marbles Greeting

This greeting moves quickly. Each student has three marbles (or other small objects). When the teacher says "Go," students mingle, greeting each other by saying, "Good morning, [classmate's name]." Every third person that a student greets gets a marble. When a student has given away all three original marbles, he or she sits down.

Make sure students have a way to distinguish their original marbles from the marbles they receive from other greeters; for example, students could hold their original marbles in their right hand. Alternatively, you could use name cards instead of marbles. Each student would have three cards with her or his name written on the cards and would give a card to every third person greeted.

Math Match Card Greeting

Prepare index cards or slips of paper, one for each student. Half should have mathematical expressions (529 – 57, 117 + 96, etc.) and half should have the corresponding answers (= 472, = 213, etc.). Give each student a card and then invite them to mix and mingle, looking for the match to their card. Matched students give each other a friendly greeting and sit down so that their equation is visible to the rest of the circle. (The student with the mathematical expression sits to the right of the student with the corresponding answer.) Going around the circle, each matched pair announce their equation while holding their cards up.

Name Card Greeting

Greetings
to Try

Place name cards upside down in a stack in the center of the circle. Turn over the top card. The student whose name is on that card begins the greeting. That student turns over the next card in the stack and greets the child whose name is on the card, taking his or her place in the circle. That child then turns over the next card, and so on. When all the cards have been used, the greeting ends with the last child greeting the first child.

One-Minute Greeting

This is a great greeting to use when time is limited. Students mingle and say, "Good morning, [classmate's name]" to as many other students as they can in one minute. So that the pace doesn't get too frantic, emphasize the importance of standing still and looking at each other with a friendly smile when greeting someone.

One, Two, Three, Four Greeting

This greeting can be sung or chanted. When a student's name is called, he comes into the circle and does whatever he wants as a movement—for example, a bow, curtsy, wave, dance, or wiggle while the rest of the class sings or chants. As the class sings the last line, the student moves back to his place in the circle. Another person's name is called and the process is repeated around the circle.

Chant:

> One, two, three, four
>
> Come on [classmate's name], hit the floor
>
> We're so glad you're here today
>
> Hurray, hurray, hurray!

Pantomime Greeting

The student who begins the greeting pantomimes something about herself (favorite activity, food, sport, etc.). The whole class then greets her by saying, "Hello, [classmate's name]" and then mimics the pantomime. Continue around the circle until all class members have been greeted.

Righty/Lefty Greeting

When you're pressed for time, this quick greeting can come in handy. One student begins by saying, "Good morning, everyone." The class responds in chorus, "Good morning." Each student then greets the person to the left and to the right (pausing as needed for each person to be available). The one important rule is that students have to look at the person they're greeting to ensure that everyone will feel welcomed and acknowledged.

Sawubona–Sikhona Greeting

This greeting uses two Zulu phrases: "Sawubona," which means "I see you," and "Sikhona," which means "I am here."

All members of the circle close their eyes. One person begins by opening her eyes, turning to the next person, and saying, "Good morning, [neighbor's first name]." That student opens his eyes and responds, "Good morning, [greeter's first name]." The first student then says "Sawubona" to the second student, who responds, "Sikhona."

The greeting continues around the circle until all have been greeted.

Greetings
to Try

Science Friction Greeting

Assign partners or have students find a partner. The pairs of students touch their palms together gently and greet each other. Next they rub their hands vigorously against their own clothes for ten seconds. Again, they touch their palms together and greet each other. Once everyone has done this, ask students for a quick reflection on what they noticed about any differences between the two greetings.

Skip Greeting

A student begins by announcing the number of spaces that everyone will skip. For example, he says "Skip four," walks around the circle to the fifth person, and greets her. The greeter then takes that person's place and sits down. The student who was greeted walks around the circle to the fifth person, greets, switches places, and sits down—and so on until everyone has been greeted. The greeting will flow around the circle several times.

Before the greeting begins, you may want to work with the class to figure out how many spaces to skip to ensure that everyone will be greeted. The last greeter (that is, the last student standing) greets the whole class, who chorally greets him back.

Snowball Greeting

Each student writes his or her name on a sheet of paper, crumples it up so that it looks like a snowball, and tosses it into the center of the circle. Everyone picks up a snowball that lands near them and opens it. A student begins the greeting by walking over to the student whose name is on her snowball and saying, "Good morning, [classmate's name]." She then returns to her place in the circle and the greeted student finds the student whose name is on his snowball, greets that student, and so on until everyone has been greeted.

VARIATION ▪ After the initial round of greetings, students recrumple the papers that they're holding and toss them. Each student picks up a new snowball, reads the name, and then respectfully observes that student for the rest of the day, with a goal of noticing something positive about the student. During a closing circle or end-of-day meeting, students pay a compliment to the classmate they observed.

Spider Web Greeting

The student who begins the greeting holds a ball of yarn. He greets someone across the circle and gently rolls or tosses the ball to that person while firmly holding on to the end of the yarn. The person who receives the ball of yarn greets another student across the circle and sends the ball to that student, making sure to hold on to the unraveling strand with one hand. This continues until everyone has been greeted and the yarn has created a web across the circle. To undo the web, students greet each other in reverse order until the ball of yarn is wound up again.

What's Your Place Value?

This greeting gives students practice with place values but can easily be adapted for other math concepts and skills. Give each student an index card or slip of paper with a three- or four-digit number on it. Choose a number (from zero through nine) and say, for example, "Anyone who has a four in the hundreds place, come to the center to meet and greet." Students who fit that description come to the center of the circle, greet each other with a friendly handshake and a "Good morning, [classmate's name]," and return to their spots in the circle. Repeat until all students have been greeted in at least one round.

Greetings to Try

Sharing

THE ART AND SKILL
OF CONVERSATION

The students in Ms. Diaz's kindergarten class have been studying nutrition. "Today," begins Ms. Diaz, "we're going to share our favorite vegetable. We'll start with Carlos and go around the circle this way." She gestures counterclockwise. "We'll use complete sentences and start each sentence with "My favorite vegetable is . . .""

She has prompted students to think about this subject ahead of Morning Meeting by asking them to draw a picture of their favorite vegetable on the day's morning message. Two picture books, *Eating the Alphabet* and *Vegetable Soup*, are propped on the chart easel, and a few children paged through the books before making their drawings.

And now they're off, naming carrots, broccoli, collard greens, cucumbers, and corn.

———

Mr. DiFranco has noticed that students choose the same classmates over and over for all kinds of activities. To help these fourth graders stretch their social circles, he has planned a partner sharing, pairing students with classmates they don't usually work or play with. "Today we're going to chat with our partners and find two things that we have in common," he instructs. "At the end, we'll share those things with the class."

Before they begin, he has students generate useful questions they might ask: What do you like to do after school? What kind of movies do you like? What do you like on your pizza? He writes the suggestions on a chart before announcing, "OK. You'll have two minutes to discover at least two things you have in common and then one more minute to pick which one you will each share with the class."

After a few minutes of lively conversation, students report back to the group. "My partner was Hollis and we discovered that we both hate anchovies on pizza, but we like pepperoni," says Hugo. "And," adds Hollis, "we both have younger brothers." Next, it is Nora's turn. "My partner was Aiden," she begins. "We both like roller coasters . . ."

As part of a study of bridges, first graders in Ms. Berkner's class have made models. They've also been working on providing supporting details in their writing and speaking. To celebrate completion of the bridge models and to practice use of supporting details, the students are taking turns individually sharing about their bridge model work with the class. A few students are sharing each day.

When it's Zachary's turn to share, he carefully transports the blue cardboard box lid that holds his construction—a truss bridge and the landscape in which it sits. He places the bridge in front of him where everyone can see it.

"This is my bridge," he says. "I used clay and toothpicks and craft sticks. It was fun to make." He pauses before concluding, "Oh, and it's a truss bridge."

He pauses again and then says, "I'm ready for questions and comments." A few hands go up and he calls on Sam.

"What part did you make first?"

"I made the land first. Lara?"

"What was the easiest part?"

"The rocks, because you just roll a piece of clay till it looks right. Nicky?"

"What was the most fun about it?"

Zachary thinks for a few moments. The class waits. "Hmm. The deck. I liked making the bridge deck the most."

PURPOSES AND REFLECTIONS

Sharing follows greeting in Morning Meeting. During sharing students present news or information about themselves or a topic related to their studies, and classmates respond. The classroom scenes that open this chapter illustrate the three main categories of sharing.

Sharing

- Around-the-circle sharing: Everyone in the group has an opportunity to offer a brief sharing.
- Partner sharing: Students pair up to have a short conversation.
- Dialogue sharing: A few students share, one by one, and the rest of the class responds with questions and comments.

Any of these types of sharing can be focused on a social or academic topic chosen by the teacher. In dialogue sharing, the topic could also be left open, with students choosing their own topics for sharing.

Daily sharing helps students get to know each other and plays an important role in building a positive classroom community. Sharing also offers opportunities to reinforce content and skills crucial to success in school and life. When the topic is drawn from academic content (nutrition and bridge-building in the opening scenes), students are getting a content review. And no matter whether the topic is academic or social, students are learning and practicing the critical skills of clear, respectful, caring, empathic communication, whether they're presenting ideas, formulating relevant questions and comments, or responding to questions and comments.

┌─────────────────── **Purposes of Sharing** ───────────────────┐

- Helps students to know each other

- Develops important social and emotional competencies

- Teaches thinking, listening, and speaking skills

- Strengthens language development and reading success

Sharing helps students to know each other

Whereas greeting helps everyone know the names of class members, sharing goes to the next step of helping students know the people attached to the names. Through sharing, we learn about each other—who is proud to be a goalie on her soccer team, who just adopted a rescue dog, who loves *Heroes of Olympus* books.

This is true even when everyone responds to the same teacher-chosen topic. "Today we'll have partner chats about something interesting we learned from the biographies we're reading," a teacher might instruct. On another day, "Our sharing will be an around-the-circle sharing on something you're looking forward to this week." As students respond to these prompts, they reveal unique and individual information.

Often these revelations help students establish a common ground that is carried beyond the meeting, especially if we help children make—and extend—connections. "We don't have time for more comments right now, but maybe the three of you could have lunch together and talk more about your favorite sports teams," a teacher might suggest. Or when lots of students seem to agree with statements made in an around-the-circle sharing, a teacher might ask, "When would be a good time to talk more about your connections?"

This kind of gentle guidance helps students move beyond their existing circle of friends. Left to their own devices, they, like all people, tend to spend time with those with whom they're most comfortable, which limits their growth. Sharing allows students to begin with a common interest, a starting place from which to

Sharing helps children learn about each others' interests inside and outside of school.

learn about differences as well as similarities. Sharing stretches their understandings of others and encourages consideration of perspectives they might not otherwise have contemplated. This is important at all grade levels—and especially important in upper grades, when students often gravitate toward exclusive social circles.

Sharing develops important social and emotional competencies

The Collaborative for Academic, Social, and Emotional Learning (CASEL) has identified five core groups of social and emotional competencies that children need for success in school and in life. These competencies are self-awareness, self-management, social awareness, relationship skills, and responsible decision-making. Sharing helps build skills in all of these areas (CASEL, n.d.).

Self-awareness and responsible decision-making

Melanie stands to speak during an open-topic sharing. "My dad and I are going camping this weekend, just the two of us. We're going to go fishing, which is something we really love to do!"

This upcoming trip is what is most important to Melanie right now. At other times, she might have chosen to share about her interest in roller skating or a movie she had just seen. When the day's sharing topic is open, students learn about the process of choosing a topic. They practice self-awareness as they reflect on their interests and values.

Self-awareness also comes into play when students respond to a teacher-chosen topic. For example, Salome's teacher says the topic of the day's sharing is "someone who shows courage." Now Salome has to decide: Will she share about her seventy-two-year-old grandmother, always terrified of the water, who is bravely taking beginner's swimming lessons? Or will she share a story she saw on the evening news about firefighters who rescued three people from an apartment fire?

Students also need to make decisions about the appropriateness of the information they share, discerning between items suitable for the public arena and those that should stay more private. Of course, we don't assume that students will know how to make these kinds of decisions at the outset of the year; we teach them how to sort and we coach and check in throughout the year.

Self-management, social awareness, and relationship skills

In all sharing formats, sharers and listeners are taking part in a reciprocal relationship of respect and caring. For this to be successful, both parties need to learn how to manage their behaviors and feelings. Sharers need to communicate clearly, and listeners need to listen attentively and respond with insight and empathy. These are complex skills that require ongoing support and teaching.

For example, we ask the class, "What can we do to be respectful when waiting for our turn to talk?" Or we reinforce, "Everyone spoke clearly and used Audience Voices today." We brainstorm questions that listeners can ask to elicit information and show curiosity about another's news or views. We generate a list of sentence starters that help listeners focus on the person sharing and demonstrate that they want to understand the sharer's perspective and care about what the sharer is saying. With our careful scaffolding, our guiding hand while they practice, and our feedback, students develop their abilities to compose and deliver their sharing and respond to others' sharing.

Perhaps the most difficult skill to learn in this arena is that of responding effectively to others' sharing.

"I bet you feel really happy that you can get your cast taken off tomorrow."

"What's one special thing you're going to do on your trip to Florida?"

"It sounds like you really liked interviewing your grandpa and writing about him."

These questions and comments, offered by listeners to various students' sharings, say "I paid attention to you; I care about how you feel." They require seeing things from another's perspective, an ability educator Sheldon Berman (1998) calls "the linchpin in the development of social consciousness." Whether the sharing is about something momentous or a more everyday occurrence, responding well requires stepping outside our own vantage point to imagine how another person feels and using constructive words and tones in response to what he or she said.

Sharing

In a seventh grade classroom, Graham proudly shares that he had an "awesome" visit with his mother over the weekend. Graham's parents are divorced and he sees his mom only occasionally. The class listens intently while he describes his visit with her. His pleasure and excitement are evident in the details he reveals. He ends his sharing with "I'm ready for questions and comments." Slowly, carefully, several hands go up. The first questions ask for more detail.

"You said your mom gave you a present. What was it?"

"What restaurant did you go to?"

As the students get more comfortable, their questions and comments show their understanding—and their empathy.

"Do you miss your mom a lot when she leaves?"

"I think you really like seeing your mom."

"What was the best part for you?"

"I met his mom," a classmate says. "She's nice." Graham's smile is wide and proud.

This is a simple but rich exchange, filled with expressions of interest and caring.

It doesn't always go so smoothly, of course. "We got a new puppy this weekend," shares kindergartner Tessa. "I'm ready for questions and comments." Hands shoot up around the circle. Tessa calls on Allie.

"I have a dog, too, and this morning he threw up on the rug," begins Allie, turning the attention away from the sharer onto herself. She takes a breath as she prepares to launch into her tale.

Her teacher takes advantage of the pause. "Tomorrow when it's your turn to share you can tell us about your dog. Right now, can you think of a question or a comment for Tessa about her news?"

Reminded, Allie certainly can. "I bet you like to play with him," she says. And sharing is back on track.

Sharing teaches thinking, listening, and speaking skills

The research of many respected educational theorists, including Jean Piaget and Lev Vygotsky, has examined and documented the ways in which social interaction influences cognitive development (Rogoff, 1990). Though Piaget and Vygotsky describe differing models of the relationship between the social and cognitive, both recognize the importance of developing the following skills:

- Stating one's thoughts with clarity
- Listening actively and forming questions that elicit more information

These skills are crucial for students to learn if they're to be successful with academics, meet the requirements of the Common Core State Standards, and flourish in our 21st century world. The beauty of sharing is that students practice these skills in meaningful ways that are integrated with the academic, social, and emotional content of their lives.

*After a student has shared, she asks for questions
and comments from her classmates.*

Stating one's thoughts with clarity

In my own school experience, I and my classmates were asked to speak to a group only in formal, artificial situations and seldom about anything of deep interest to us. Instead, we were assigned to do "oral reports" on designated topics, reports that were thinly disguised paraphrases of encyclopedia passages. We were encouraged to speak at length, and we often mumbled to disguise the fact that we couldn't pronounce many of the words we had painstakingly copied.

How wonderfully different sharing is! First of all, the material has intrinsic interest, and students can make choices even within structured topics. A teacher says, "We're going to do an around-the-circle sharing about a fun fact you learned in our study of rivers." Although the topic is named for them, each student gets to think about and name a personally appealing snippet of information from a recent lesson.

Sharing presentations are concise. Rather than learning to pad a presentation to stretch it out, students must synthesize information and then share enough to pique interest and give their audience a basis for response, while leaving room and reason for further inquiry and comment.

In small, low-stakes doses, sharing provides everyday practice in speaking to groups of different sizes. For example, students must speak in clear, audible voices when addressing the whole group; they must modulate the volume when engaging in partner chats. When students can't hear a speaker, we teach a polite signal for "turn up the volume," and they practice assertiveness when they use it.

Finally, to present their sharing to classmates, students must be able to choose words that convey information clearly and to craft and deliver a comprehensible narrative. When they don't, the feedback is immediate.

"Wait a minute. I'm confused. When you say California is the biggest state, do you mean a lot of land or a lot of people?" Jared asks his classmate, Ruben, after Ruben has shared about the state he is studying. Ruben says, "I mean a lot of people," and then, after a pause, "So I guess I should say California is the most populous state." Ruben and the whole class have just gotten a mini-lesson on choosing precise words.

Listening actively and forming questions that elicit more information

Being a productive member of the class during sharing requires that students listen to and remember what others say so that they can respond appropriately. Since the topics often spring from their direct experience, students are motivated to engage in the conversations, to hear each other.

Teachers also teach students that it's their job as listeners to formulate a question that elicits more information, or to make a comment that shows interest in the news presented or concern for the sharer—habits important for learning and for building relationships.

When Sadia asks Marcus, "How did you get the color in the flames to look so much like a real fire?" Marcus knows that Sadia has carefully observed his painting and that she really listened when he said that he was proud of the way he had blended colors in it.

Sharing strengthens language development and reading success

Through Morning Meeting sharing, students build vocabulary, learn pronunciation, and learn to speak with grammatical accuracy. Equally as important, the conversations that take place during sharing help build students' background knowledge of a wide variety of topics, and that background knowledge helps them make sense of text when reading. In fact, researchers have recognized that all the conversational skills children learn and practice during Morning Meeting sharing—starting conversations, telling stories, listening, asking questions, commenting—are essential to literacy success (Goodson & Layzer, 2009; Zwiers & Crawford, 2011).

Some students may not recognize all of the words used during sharing conversations. In that case, teachers can define the words or help students use context clues to figure out words they don't know. Sometimes they spot and correct students' misunderstandings, as in the following third-grade example.

"On Saturday I went to Adventure World with my uncle. I went swimming there and I drowned," shares Regina.

Her classmates are full of questions about her trip.

"How long did it take to get there?"

"Was there traffic?"

"Was it scary when you drowned?"

Wide-eyed and solemn, Regina nods emphatically. "It was really scary."

Her teacher has listened and observed closely, and notices that many of the children share the same misunderstanding of this part of Regina's news.

"Regina," she asks, "when you said that you drowned, did you mean that you had trouble swimming in the water?"

Regina nods yes. An impromptu vocabulary lesson follows, a thread picked up from the fabric of Regina's sharing and woven seamlessly into the classroom circle.

"Drowned is connected to having trouble in the water," affirms the teacher, "but it means that you had so much trouble that you died from not being able to get your face above the water to breathe."

The class listens intently. No embarrassment is attached to the mistake; they are glad to receive this information, given succinctly and matter-of-factly. It extends their ability to describe their own experiences and to interpret the experiences of others accurately in both oral communication and future texts they may encounter.

Highlights of Sharing

- Provides an arena for students to share news and views

- Lets students learn about each other

- Offers practice in speaking to a partner and to a group

- Develops students' judgment of the appropriateness of sharing various kinds of news with different audiences

- Allows students to practice careful listening

- Offers students an engaging way to develop empathy, consideration of others' perspectives, and social awareness

- Helps students develop a repertoire of responses to different kinds of news, including asking constructive, purposeful questions and offering empathic, insightful comments

- Enhances students' vocabulary development and reading success

Before continuing on to the next section, you may want to browse through Sharing Ideas to Try starting on page 119.

Simple around-the-circle sharings are a good way to start Morning Meeting sharing early in the year.

GETTING STARTED

Introduce around-the-circle and partner sharing first

It's the second day of school and the fourth graders have just finished a simple greeting. I wait until everyone is quiet and say, "Today we're going to do sharing. I'm going to ask a question. We'll go around the circle and each of you will have a chance to answer the question. Who has done this kind of sharing in third grade?"

Several hands shoot up. "OK. Today you will state one key idea in response to my question 'What is one thing you enjoy doing outside?' First, watch and notice what I do and say. 'Outside, I like to play catch with my son.' What did you notice about my sharing?"

Students respond, noticing that I stuck to the key idea, spoke loudly, looked around the circle, and limited my sharing to only one sentence and one idea. These are all important skills, but for the purpose of this first sharing, I'm most interested in having students keep their statements brief. This can be a difficult skill for loquacious fourth graders.

After I model, I reinforce the "one idea" expectation by saying, "Take a minute and think. What is one thing you enjoy doing outside? When you're ready, give a thumbs-up."

While children are thinking, to remind them of the "one sentence" goal I post a chart with a sentence stem on it: "Outside, I like to _____." As soon as all thumbs are up, we begin. I go first: "Outside, I like to play baseball with my three children." I turn to Carly on my left. "Carly, you're next." And the first day of sharing proceeds around the room.

Sharing is an essential part of Morning Meeting, introduced in the first days of school. In these early days, sharing is highly structured. Many teachers do around-the-circle sharing as a first experience. In around-the-circle sharing, as the example above shows, all members of the meeting circle share about a teacher-chosen topic. The around-the-circle structure provides a safe way to introduce basic sharing skills: how to decide on an idea to share, how to speak clearly, how to listen attentively and remember what was shared.

Other teachers might choose to do partner sharing first. In partner sharing, students pair up to talk with each other on a teacher-chosen topic. This is a good choice for a first sharing experience if a teacher has many students who are shy about speaking in front of the group or who might get wiggly while others are speaking. Whether they begin with around-the-circle or partner sharing, teachers set the parameters carefully and provide ample support and guidance.

Introduce dialogue sharing as students' skills grow

As students' skills and comfort levels grow, teachers introduce dialogue sharing, in which one person shares news or information with the entire class and then asks for questions and comments. To be successful with dialogue sharing, students need to share a main idea and supporting details, speak clearly, listen carefully, and offer thoughtful questions and comments.

Because dialogue sharing tends to be the hardest for students, it's usually the last format introduced, and the skills are taught gradually. Sometimes teachers use partner sharing as a bridge to dialogue sharing because partner sharing allows students to learn and practice many of the skills they'll need for dialogue sharing in a lower-risk format. Initially, the class does dialogue sharing on a teacher-chosen topic (also called a focused topic). Later, they move to dialogue sharing with an open topic.

Throughout the year, choose the format that best suits students' needs

Once the class is competent in all formats, teachers choose which format to use on a given day depending on students' needs, time constraints, and classroom events. For example, on a day when the teacher wants everyone to think and talk about a certain topic, he might use around-the-circle sharing. I have found that this is a good format for Mondays when students are excited about weekend activities or caught up in current events that happened while they were apart.

On a subsequent day, partner sharing or dialogue sharing might provide a time for more in-depth conversations. For example, students could do a partner sharing or a focused-topic dialogue sharing about which book character they like best and why.

There's no prescription for how to pick and choose among these three formats as the year unfolds. Many teachers focus on dialogue sharing, recognizing that this format provides deep practice in speaking, listening, and thinking skills. Others might find that around-the-circle sharing or partner sharing most frequently suits students' needs. The bottom line is to do sharing in a way that offers an appropriate level of challenge and that allows all class members to feel heard and cared for in a safe environment.

Teach sharing skills: Jobs of the sharer

Sharing is complex, even in the highly structured around-the-circle and partner formats. Students need to think about what to say, formulate a complete and focused thought, and articulate it clearly. They also need to exert enough self-

*Sharing goes more smoothly when teachers explicitly teach
both the jobs of the sharer and the jobs of the listener.*

control to sit quietly while others talk, and they need to focus attention on the speaker. For these reasons it's important to break sharing down into its component skills and to carefully teach each skill. All grade levels benefit from this explicit teaching—upper grades teachers might assume that older students already know how to share and listen, but often they don't.

The jobs of the sharer include using a strong, clear voice, looking at the audience, and saying something brief, focused, and on topic. In the fourth grade around-the-circle sharing described above, I began by teaching how to state one key idea. In subsequent days, I focused on speaking in a clear and audible voice; choosing appropriate, on-topic items to share; looking around at the entire audience, not just one person; using facial expression; and stating a main idea with supporting details.

Interactive Modeling is a key strategy to use in teaching all of these skills (see pages 26–27 for more information about Interactive Modeling).

Following are some other strategies you might use to support students as they learn sharing skills.

Brainstorm for ideas

When you first introduce sharing on a focused topic, ask students to brainstorm possible responses. To give students some ideas to draw on, write their ideas on a chart before starting the sharing. For example, in a first grade classroom, we brainstormed a list of favorite everyday places before doing an around-the-circle sharing. This served two purposes—it helped children stay on topic, and it enabled me to guide children in naming truly everyday places such as "my grandma's kitchen" or "our back porch."

Use sentence stems

Posting a sentence stem that children complete will help them focus and also support them in learning to use complete sentences. This is especially useful in younger grades and with ELL students. In a K–1 class, the sentence stem may be as simple as "A healthy food I like is _____." Sentence stems can also help older students stay on topic and formulate complex sentences. In a seventh grade class, the sentence stem might be: "I connected with the character _____ from our book because _____."

Sharing

Give clear directions

Setting clear parameters in your directions can help students stay focused. Instead of saying, "Tell about your animal habitat project," you can narrow things down by saying, "Tell one important part of your animal habitat project."

Use think-alouds

To model how to choose one idea among many, you might do a "think-aloud." Use a gesture such as putting a finger to your head to indicate that you're going to speak your thoughts and then narrate a thought process. Let's say the topic is "What I like to do on weekends." Your think-aloud might sound like this: "Hmm . . . I like to do lots of different things. I like to go to the farmer's market, sometimes I go to the movies, and it's fun to go walking in the park because I can take my dog. I know some of the other kids have dogs—maybe that's what I'll share."

Teach sharing skills: Jobs of the listener

In all forms of sharing, listeners need to stay quiet, maintain self-control, and demonstrate attentive listening. As the class's sophistication with sharing evolves, listeners need to remember what was said, formulate questions that show interest and elicit more information, and make empathic comments.

Here is a possible sequence of skills to teach. Introduce each skill as students show readiness to take their sharing to the next level of complexity.

Remembering details

Before students begin an around-the-circle sharing, tell them to listen carefully to what their classmates say because they'll be playing "Who Remembers?" afterward. Give them a minute to think of a strategy they can use to remember what is said. Then, when everyone has shared, ask questions to prompt recall. For example, if the sharing was about a favorite book, ask questions such as "Who remembers whose favorite book was *Twister on Tuesday*?" or "Who remembers who named a nonfiction book as their favorite?" When the class has done this activity a few times, you could ask students to come up with the "Who remembers?" questions.

As a next step, have listeners remember details of what was shared during partner sharing or focused-topic dialogue sharing. For example, one typical morning when I was teaching fourth grade, after Serena finished a dialogue sharing about teaching her dog new tricks, I said, "Raise your hand if you can name one thing you heard Serena say." Students responded, "Her dog's name is Marley." "Her dog is 12 years old." "She taught her dog two new tricks." "One of the tricks she taught her dog was how to shake." Students continued to respond until they had named all the things they'd heard Serena say.

A variation on remembering details is to ask listeners to summarize what the sharer said. You can introduce this variation during partner sharing using an assigned topic. Each partner shares about the topic and then, going around the circle, students take turns summarizing for the whole group what their partner said.

Generating effective questions

Effective questions reflect the spirit of sharing—they acknowledge and encourage the sharer. You can introduce the skill of asking questions during a partner sharing—when students will be asking questions to learn about each other—or during a dialogue sharing. Begin by discussing what makes an effective question. Be sure the following points are covered:

- Effective questions show interest in the sharer and her news.

- They can be about either the factual or the emotional content of the sharing.

- They often elicit new information and extend understanding.

- They sometimes clarify information.

- They are positive and supportive rather than challenging.

Next, post a list of question words (see sample chart above) and give students an opportunity to practice using them. You could share a quick story or an opinion about a topic the class is interested in and then have them use the question words to generate questions about what they heard.

Question Words

Who	Who helped you with that?
	Did someone help you figure that out?
What	What was your favorite part about _____?
	What made you excited [happy, sad] about that?
When	When do you think you will _____?
	When would you like to _____?
Where	Where were you when this happened?
	Where did this take place?
Why	Why do you think _____?
	Why did you decide to _____?
How	How did you feel about that?
	How did he [she, they] respond when you _____?

Sharing

Finally, remind and encourage students to use the question words during partner sharing or dialogue sharing. When you first introduce question-asking during dialogue sharing with younger students, help them along by having the class pause before the sharer invites questions. As a class, brainstorm possible questions using the question words you've posted. Then return to the sharing format and let the sharer signal they are ready for questions. With older students, you could simply refer to a posted list of question starters to remind them of the kinds of questions to ask.

With older students, I have also used a sticky note strategy: After a student shares, I pass out a sticky note and pencil to each student. Working with a partner, they each write down an interesting question to ask (being sure to sign the note) and give the note to the sharer. The sharer then chooses three or four questions to answer aloud; remaining questions are posted on a sharing chart by the circle area to be answered individually when the sharer has time.

Making empathic comments

Making empathic comments offers unique opportunities for students to practice important academic and social skills. Students need to listen attentively; observe and interpret a classmate's words, body language, and tone; remember what was said; and formulate a relevant and respectful observation or affirmation.

Of all the skills involved in sharing, offering empathic comments is perhaps the hardest to learn. It requires taking another's perspective and thinking about what will help that person feel heard and cared for. Because this ability develops as children mature, younger children tend to have more difficulty offering comments than older children. (There are, however, developmental exceptions. Thirteen-year-olds, for example, can be intensely self-focused and often have difficulty thinking of empathic comments.)

Here's a suggested sequence for introducing commenting:

Offering empathic comments requires taking another's perspective and thinking about what will help that person feel heard and cared for.

Sharing

1 *Discuss what a comment is and what makes a good comment.* ▪ Make sure the following points are made:

- Takes the form of a statement rather than a question.
- Helps the sharer feel listened to and supported.
- Focuses on the sharer rather than on the responder; this point is especially important for younger students, who are usually eager to share their own experiences in response to a classmate's sharing ("I have a puppy, too!").
- Might notice and appreciate a detail from the sharing.
- Might respond to how the sharer feels; listeners will need to pay attention to body language, facial expression, and tone along with words so that they can make comments of this type.

2 *Brainstorm empathic comments.* ▪ Briefly share something with the class, being sure to convey emotion along with interesting detail. For example, here is a story I shared with students: "Late yesterday afternoon when I was starting to make dinner for my family, I heard a loud bang and heard my daughter scream. I ran toward the front door and she told me that our dog had figured out how to open the front door and was loose in the neighborhood. There's a busy street nearby and I was worried that Shennah might be heading that way. I ran all over the neighborhood and was so relieved when I finally found her at the park chasing some squirrels."

After telling your story, ask students to brainstorm a list of comments that either note details about what you said or note how you felt, being sure to keep the focus on you and your news. As students brainstorm, write their sentence starters on a chart: "You must have felt . . ." "I bet you were really wondering . . ." "It sounds like you . . ." "I can tell that you . . ."

Then ask students what these comments have in common. They'll probably soon discover that all the comments include the word "you"—in other words, the focus stays on the sharer. Keep this chart posted by the meeting circle for students to use as a reference.

3 *Separate questions from comments at the next Morning Meeting.* ▪ At the next meeting, do a dialogue sharing and bring in commenting, but keep it separate from question-asking. Have the class brainstorm a list of comments in response to each sharing. Then, after all comments have been voiced, sharers can say, "I am ready for questions."

4 *Model and practice how to respond respectfully to a comment.* ▪ Just as it's important for listeners to offer empathic comments, it's important that sharers respond respectfully to those comments. Model how to do this. For example, for the loose dog story, I might go back to the class's brainstormed comments and give some respectful responses: "Yes, I was feeling really worried about my dog; I thought a car might have hit her," "I do feel lucky that nothing happened to her," or just a simple "Thank you" perhaps along with a nod. After your modeling, give students a chance to practice respectfully acknowledging a comment.

5 *Put it all together.* ▪ The final step is to have the audience give both comments and questions during partner and dialogue sharing. Listeners now need to incorporate all the questioning and commenting skills they've practiced, and sharers must deploy all they've learned about answering questions and responding to comments.

Sharing Skills to Teach, Model, and Practice	
Introduce during around-the-circle sharing	▪ Speak in a clear voice ▪ Look at the audience when speaking ▪ State one main idea ▪ Stay on topic ▪ Listen quietly and respectfully while others are speaking ▪ Remember details of what was shared
Introduce during partner sharing	▪ State one main idea with supporting details ▪ Ask friendly questions to elicit more information ▪ Make empathic comments
Introduce during dialogue sharing	▪ Sign up to share ▪ Choose appropriate topics for open-topic sharing ▪ Initiate questions and comments ▪ As audience member, raise hand to speak and speak only when called on

Pay attention to the focus and flow of sharing

An important teacher role during sharing is to help students stay focused and maintain a comfortable conversational give-and-take. In around-the-circle sharing, teachers often need to help the class stay on topic. You can proactively address this by being clear about the topic and by modeling—and re-modeling—how to share one key idea. When individuals do stray off topic or start to share a whole story, remind them of the topic and the one-idea limit.

In dialogue sharing, common challenges are making sure that all sharers get responses and that all students, rather than the same few, offer questions and

*Children listen more carefully when they are expected
to formulate questions and comments.*

comments. If you notice problems in these areas, it's important to address them directly and give students a chance to think about and practice the skills involved.

For example, I might begin by naming the problem: "Although sharing has been interesting, sharers haven't been getting many questions and comments." I would then lead a brief discussion to build empathy for how actions, intentional or not, can make someone feel. "How does it feel when you're sharing and only a couple of people raise their hands with questions or comments?" After taking a few responses, I name my expectation for all: "I know it can be hard sometimes to come up with questions and comments in the moment, but that is the job of the audience."

I remind sharers that they need to use a phrase such as "I am ready for questions and comments" rather than asking if there are any questions. This signals the expectation that there will be questions and comments. I would then give a refresher lesson: Just as when I first taught the class about questioning and commenting, I share something interesting with the class and have them brainstorm and practice offering both questions and comments.

Importantly, I'd end on an encouraging note, reinforcing students' efforts during the lesson and reiterating my expectations for future sharing: "Wow. We brainstormed eleven questions and seven comments. The rest of this week, I'll be watching for all of you to be thinking hard about what else would be interesting to find out from sharers and what thoughtful responses you can offer them."

Direct the content of sharing as needed to keep it inclusive

It's important to take an active role in directing the content of sharing, even—or especially—when it is open-topic sharing. Obviously we don't want to stifle children from sharing about special events in their lives, but we do want to avoid having them share things that highlight advantages and shut out less-advantaged classmates.

One way we can address this is by helping students identify and share about topics that don't involve objects or special opportunities based on economics. For example, after winter break I might have students share about "a favorite memory" or "a special time you spent with someone" rather than "a favorite gift."

An eighth grade teacher even used Morning Meeting sharing time to have her students discuss the issue of economics and the holidays head-on. In an around-the-circle sharing in early December, she asked the class, "Do you have to give something expensive for a gift to be valuable? What's one idea of a gift you could give that doesn't cost anything?" Later she reflected: "I was so moved by their responses. A lot of these kids' families don't have much money. They came up with wonderful ideas! Things that they could make, things that they already had and would like to share. They suggested the gift of time—of being there to really listen to someone."

In classes of younger children, the "Bring and Brag" syndrome is often a problem throughout the year. Many teachers avoid this by establishing a general "no toys for sharing" rule. Recognizing, however, that sometimes it's important to have a chance to share a special item, other teachers occasionally do "category sharing"—choosing a category of things that they're sure most children will have, for example, "Bring Your Favorite Stuffie Week" or "Bring Something You Liked to Play With as a Baby Week."

Teach students what news is appropriate to share with the class

For the purposes of Morning Meeting, teach students to sort the news in their lives into two overall categories—community news and private family news.

Community news is appropriate for the classroom community to hear; private family news is not appropriate for sharing with the whole class. The latter category could include information that is confidential from a legal or ethical viewpoint or details a child has overheard about a court case a family member is involved in, or it might include a complicated family situation, such as a divorce or family dispute.

Let students know that they can share private family news with you, their teacher, but not the whole class. Making this distinction not only protects the student and the family but also protects the rest of the class from access to information that is beyond their capacity to cope with or understand.

Reassure students that sometimes it's hard to decide whether certain news is suitable for group sharing, and make sure they know that if in doubt, they should check in with you. One teacher tells her class, "If something is really troubling you, it might upset other students as well. Talk to me before you share information like this with the class."

Also helpful is brainstorming a list of appropriate news items and posting the list near the meeting circle. You can then refer students to this list as they prepare to do open-topic dialogue sharing. I might begin such a brainstorming session by asking, "If sharing is a time to get to know each other better, what types of information might you share?" Students list things such as hobbies, family, pets, books they like, something especially interesting they learned recently at school, something they learned at school that they have questions about, a special memory, friends. We would continue adding ideas to this chart throughout the year.

Finally, if a student begins to share news that you realize is inappropriate, intervene. For example, Katy's mother is a reporter for the town newspaper. One day, Katy began to share details of a recent crime that she'd heard her mother talk about. Knowing that this was straying into dicey territory, the teacher stopped her. "Katy, I'd like you to hold on to the rest of your sharing until I can talk with you about it later. I'm not sure that it's news for our whole class to hear." She then made sure to talk with Katy soon after the meeting.

Prepare students to handle the sharing of serious news

Within the "community news" category—news that's appropriate for the class—are often light, humorous, or matter-of-fact topics. But community news might also be sad and painful or worrisome. When the classroom climate is safe and comfortable, both kinds of news can be offered and received with care and respect.

Younger children tend to blurt out what they need to say when they need to say it. With the help of their teacher, however, they are able to recognize that some news is serious and demands a different kind of response than other, lighter news. As teachers, we can model a response: "I'm sorry to hear that your dad is in the hospital."

Older children can be more deliberate about the sharing of serious news. Some teachers of older children introduce labels for the two types of community news—newsy news and serious news, for example. When a class first begins doing Morning Meeting sharing, most news offered tends to be newsy news. When class members are at ease with the structures of sharing, questions, and comments, and when they trust each other to respond easily and respectfully to newsy news, you might inform the group that they are ready to add serious news.

Sharing

Emphasize to students that they should always bring serious news to you first and you will determine whether it's appropriate to share with the group. In some cases, you may need to help a student modify the serious news to make it appropriate; in other cases, you may need to explain to a student that the news is not suitable to share with the class. Let parents know ahead of time that you will be introducing serious news and that you will be carefully filtering any serious news the students bring in.

Through discussion and brainstorming, help the class sort and categorize their news. What are some examples of newsy news? Serious news? It's also helpful to generate ideas for constructive responses to different kinds of news: "If someone shares something sad," you might ask, "what can we say to let them know that we listened well and that we care how they feel?"

These are not skills commonly taught. Even as well-intentioned adults, we often struggle to find the "right" words. Too often, our awkwardness and discomfort can cause us to avoid acknowledging another's pain or offering our help. The practice provided by responding to news during sharing can help students feel more competent at navigating these situations.

Make sure questions and comments are caring and empathic

An incident in a first grade classroom highlights the importance of the teacher's role in directing the tone of questions and comments, be they in response to serious, light-hearted, excited, or matter-of-fact sharings.

It was December, only a few days before the holiday vacation, and the six-year-olds in Ms. Donnelly's classroom were spilling over with the excitement of the season.

When the time came for dialogue sharing, Anthony was the first to share. His words flew out fast and excited. "My grandma's coming from Italy to visit me!"

"He already told us that!" blurted Adam. It was a thoroughly six-year-old retort, impulsive and tinged with righteous indignation at having to hear something twice. It was not meant to be unkind, though it fell with a cruel thud upon the enthusiastic Anthony.

Instead of directly chastising Adam, Ms. Donnelly asked a question. "Why might Anthony want to tell us again that his grandma is coming? What would make a person repeat news?"

Several ideas were ventured. "I say things twice when I'm really excited!"

"Maybe Anthony's got more to tell than when he told it the first time."

"Probably 'cause it's really important news to him."

Ms. Donnelly nodded and then handed the reins back to Anthony. "OK, Anthony, you can choose people for questions and comments." Questions abounded:

"How long since you saw her?"

"When's she coming?"

"Is she gonna bring you a present from Italy?"

Ms. Donnelly made the final comment. "Maybe, Anthony, your grandma could come to school with you."

Without the guidance of their teacher, this group of six-year-olds would probably have been unable to move beyond their concern about the detail of Adam's observation into a contemplation based upon empathy for Anthony. More likely, their diversion into "who said what when" would have prevented them from responding to Anthony's news at all.

The teacher's intervention and response to Adam's comment let the whole class know that the important thing was to think about Anthony and respond to his news in a caring way. But she did this in a way that did not highlight Adam or his blunder. He stood corrected, but gently and quickly, giving him space to learn from his mistake. Moreover, because Ms. Donnelly invited everyone to help solve the puzzle of why a person might share the same news twice, the discovery was not limited to the two children directly involved but instead became a spontaneous, whole-class lesson in empathy and understanding people's motivations.

Sharing Responsibilities

In implementing and assessing sharing, keep the following general responsibilities in mind.

Teachers' Responsibilities

- Set up systems for dialogue sharing, such as signing up ahead of time on a schedule chart, and designating the number of questions and comments allowed.

- Keep the process moving by acting as facilitator and timekeeper.

- Model good oral communication skills.

- Model appropriate language for questions and comments.

- Help students keep the focus on the sharer.

- Screen out or stop sharing that is inappropriate for the group.

Students' Responsibilities

- Choose news that is appropriate to share with the group.

- Organize their ideas and keep their sharing brief.

- Speak loudly and clearly.

- Look at their audience.

- Wait their turn to share.

- Put any objects they'll need for their sharing in the designated "sharing" place to avoid distracting themselves or others.

- Listen attentively when others are sharing.

- Offer questions and comments that are focused on the sharer and that show interest, respect, and caring.

- Respond appropriately to questions and comments.

Teachers facilitate sharing and make sure all students are heard.

FINE TUNINGS

Q What should I do when a student doesn't speak loudly enough for others to hear or when the class can't understand a particular child? Should I repeat that child's words?

ANSWER ▪ Though these situations call for individual judgment, a general guideline is to resist "voice-overs." Allow sharers to speak for themselves unless a severe speech problem or some other issue clearly creates communication difficulties. Make sure students know and use courteous ways of telling a classmate that they didn't hear or understand something that was said.

I struggled with this issue when I taught second graders, who tend to be quiet and unassertive. I wanted to empower children to take charge of their own learning and to communicate when they couldn't hear or understand what someone was saying. We created a "turn it up" signal that anyone could use (extend your arm, make a fist with thumb to the side then turn your fist so the thumb points up). And when children heard but didn't understand another child's words, they would say, "Could you repeat that, please? I didn't catch all your words."

Q Is it all right for me to ask questions and make comments or should I leave that to the students?

ANSWER ▪ It is definitely all right for you to ask questions and offer comments. In fact, it's vital for students to see that you find their news interesting and that you care about how things are going for them. It's also a good opportunity to model questions and comments in an unobtrusive way.

However, it's best to allow students to respond first. Also, avoid responding to every single sharing. If you do, the message is that an exchange isn't really valid unless the teacher has spoken.

Q I know I should discourage responses that shift the focus onto the responder—comments like "I have a cat too, and . . ." But sometimes these seem like honest attempts at connection and empathy, not simple self-centeredness. Is it ever OK to allow such comments?

ANSWER ▪ This question involves a judgment call we must make as we guide sharing. Is the intention of the response to highlight a connection with the sharer and acknowledge a bond revealed by the sharing? Or is the intention to divert the focus from the sharer to the responder and his or her news?

Like many distinctions, this is not always clear and tidy. What begins as an acknowledgment of connection can slide quickly into one's own sharing. When that happens, the teacher needs to stop the commenting child with a respectful reminder: "That sounds like some interesting information about you, Chris. You could share it tomorrow when it's your turn. Now you can ask Bruce a question or make a comment about his sharing."

The goal is to help students respond to another's experience without bringing the attention back to themselves. I often tell them that we want to "keep the spotlight on the sharer." Some teachers model and practice with students a specific signal to use that indicates "I have a connection with you." Along with teaching a signal, you can also discuss times students could talk more about shared interests and experiences. For example, ask students, "When might be a good time to talk about our connections? What could you say if you wanted to talk to someone later in the day about your shared interest?"

Q **When children bring in an object to share, they often can't find it when it's their turn to share. Or everyone in the circle wants to touch the object. Sometimes arguments occur over how the object is handled. How can I keep the child's sharing from getting lost in the shuffle?**

ANSWER ▪ Sharing objects can create lots of problems in addition to the "Bring and Brag" syndrome previously discussed. If you're going to have children bring in objects for sharing, you can use various strategies to keep the objects from becoming distractions. One is to designate a "Show Shelf" or "Sharing Basket" in the room. When children bring in an object for sharing, they leave it in this spot where others are able to view it but not touch it.

Once the object is shared, it's put back on the shelf until the end of the day. If the sharer wants children to handle the object later in the day, the sharer can explain and demonstrate during sharing how the object should be handled. Finally, as a general rule, don't allow objects to be passed around the circle. It usually takes a very long time, during which the focus is shifted from the sharer to the object itself.

Q **Sharing can be daunting to many ELL students. Some are nervous about needing to comprehend their classmates and even more nervous about speaking in front of them. How can I support them while keeping sharing meaningful for the rest of the class?**

ANSWER ▪ Around-the-circle sharing provides a lot of support and allows students to hear many similar statements on the same topic. In partner sharing, students need to speak in front of only one person, which reduces risk. But even dialogue sharing can be manageable for ELL students with some simple supports. Following are a few ideas.

Use rehearsal

Sharing doesn't need to be spontaneous speech. You or other students in the class can work with ELL students outside of Morning Meeting to help them prepare for sharing.

Use sentence starters or fill-in-the-blank cues

Let's say you're doing a focused-topic sharing in which students choose three things to tell about themselves, for example, "I like math. I have a guinea pig. I play basketball." To make this easier, you can give students a fill-in-the-blank sentence format: "I like to eat _____. I come from _____. My favorite color is _____."

Use props

Plan sharings in which students bring in a photo or other item from home, hold it up, and then respond to questions. At first, you can restrict the questions to simple yes-or-no questions. As students begin to learn vocabulary, the supportive environment of sharing will give them wonderful opportunities to practice speaking and to gain fluency.

Share classwork

Sharing class projects or artwork is a simple way for ELL students to participate in sharing. Before Morning Meeting, they can work with the teacher or a classmate to prepare and practice brief descriptive statements about the project or artwork.

SHARING IDEAS TO TRY

The sharing ideas on the folllowing pages are flexible: They can be adapted for a range of ages and purposes and for different times of the year. Feel free to use them as is or modify them to meet students' needs.

Grade level

Most of the ideas can be used at multiple grade levels, with modifications in the level of challenge. For example, in the around-the-circle sharing Favorites (page 120), younger students might be most successful responding with a word or simple phrase, whereas older students could use complete sentences and perhaps add information about why something is a favorite.

Time of year

Ideas that work well for older students early in the year might not be appropriate for younger students until mid-year or later, when they've had time to learn basic sharing skills and any relevant content knowledge. For example, if you teach older students, you might use Mix and Mingle (page 125) to pair them up right from the beginning of the year. But if you teach younger students, you might want to wait until later in the year when they've had more opportunities to practice self-control and responding to signals for quiet.

Purpose

With some modification, the same sharing idea can be used to meet a range of academic and social purposes. For example, you can use the What We Have in Common partner chat (page 126) to have students name common questions they have about some recently learned content or name common interests they have outside of school.

---   **Around-the-Circle Sharing**   ---

Class Rocks

Ask students to bring in a small rock that they find outside or near their home. Give students practice in observation by challenging them to notice their rock's characteristics (for example, texture, color, grain size). Going around the circle, each student presents their rock, tells where they found it, and names one characteristic about it. Model the sharing: "I found this rock in a park near my home. It has a smooth texture."

After everyone has shared, ask reflective questions that help students practice comparison and categorization skills: What did you notice about our rocks? What do our rocks have in common? How might we sort these rocks into groups?

Favorites

Name a category such as vegetables, colors, numbers, foods, games, books, or songs (you can write a question on the morning message chart to preview the category: "Be ready to share a favorite _____ during Morning Meeting.").

Going around the circle, each student names a favorite item in the chosen category. Depending on age and skill level, students can use just one word, a short phrase, or a complete sentence. Model how to do the sharing. When students are first using complete sentences, you can post a sentence stem for added support: My favorite vegetable is _____.

After a student shares, invite the rest of the class to make the "Me, too!" sign if they like the same thing (fold down the middle three fingers; move hand with thumb and pinkie extended back and forth toward the sharer and yourself).

To extend this sharing, tally the favorites and use the data for a graphing activity later.

Headlines!

In advance, give students index cards and invite them to write a headline about themselves (for example, "This Weekend Brings a Surprise Visitor"; "*Bud, Not Buddy* Is a Favorite Book"; "Family Reunion Planned for Next Summer"). Students should not put their names on their cards. At the meeting, collect and shuffle the cards and pass out one to each student.

Going around the circle, each student reads aloud the headline on their card and guesses who wrote it. If a student doesn't guess correctly after a couple of tries, the headline writer stands and says, "That's me!" After everyone has read a card, prompt students to learn more about their classmates during other times of the school day, for example, lunch and recess.

If I Were One Inch Tall

A fun prelude to this sharing is to read Shel Silverstein's poem "One Inch Tall" with the class. For the sharing, each student completes the sentence, "If I were one inch tall, I would _____." Challenge students to be inventive and thoughtful in their responses. Model an example, such as "If I were one inch tall, I would use a toothpick as a vaulting pole."

VARIATION ▪ Before students start to share, let them know that you'll play a quick game of "Who Remembers?" right after everyone has shared. Ask questions such as "Who remembers someone who shared what they would eat?" "Who remembers someone who shared what they would do outside?"

VARIATION ▪ Use other measurements ("If I were one centimeter tall . . ." "If I were one meter tall . . .").

It Could Be a . . .

In the middle of the circle, display several shapes that students have been learning about in math. Write a sentence frame on a chart or interactive whiteboard: "I know this is a _____ [shape], but it could be a _____ [item that has that shape]." Choose one shape and model the sharing. For example: "I know this is a cylinder, but it could be my new pencil holder." Then go around the circle, with each student choosing a shape and doing a similar sharing.

VARIATION ▪ Before you begin, let students know that you'll be asking them to remember what their classmates shared. Right after the last sharer, ask questions to see how many different ideas the class can remember for each shape and list those on a chart. Encourage students to add new ideas to the chart throughout the day.

Something I Learned . . .

Each student names a "fun fact" from a recent lesson (specify the subject matter and lesson before the sharing) and says one thing about why they chose that fact. After each student shares, the rest of the class has an opportunity to make a connection using the "Me, too!" sign (see Favorites on page 120).

Model the sharing. For a lesson on colonial life, you might say: "I learned that most girls or women did not go to school during colonial times but were instead taught skills needed for running a house and farm and raising children. I think this is interesting because I can't imagine not having the chance to go to school to get an education and I would feel upset about not having the same opportunities as boys."

For added support, you can post sentence stems: I just learned _____. I think this is interesting because _____.

Give students some think time. When they're ready to share, have them show thumbs-up. Take the first turn yourself and then go around the circle, with each student sharing and classmates giving the "Me, too!" sign.

What Can We Share About?

Let the class know that they'll be identifying topics that they can share about throughout the year. Provide examples of appropriate topics—for example, favorite foods, favorite games, pets, a piece of schoolwork. Go around the circle, with each student suggesting one topic. Write ideas on a chart, redirecting as needed if anyone names an inappropriate topic. Post this list in the meeting circle and add to it as new topics arise.

Years of Trash

Ahead of time, tell students to bring an item of trash from their home or neighborhood. The item should be safe and sanitary, likely to last for 100 years in a landfill, and represent something about themselves or their family or community. Brainstorm suitable examples, such as product packaging, used gift cards, and rinsed-out soft drink cans. You may want to keep some extra items on hand for students who forget to bring something.

Model how to share: "I chose this water bottle. I think it will last 100 years in a landfill because it's made of plastic. I see a lot of people drinking water from bottles like these when I go to the gym."

As students share, you can list items or put them all in a bin for later use. If students disagree with someone's prediction of what will be in the landfill in 100 years, tell them to hold their thoughts because they'll have time for discussion later in the day. At that time, they can also discuss how to make a more sustainable choice for each item rather than adding it to the landfill, such as using a reusable bottle for water.

**Sharing
Ideas to Try**

——————————————— **Partner Sharing** ———————————————

Structures for Pairing Up

You can use these structures for many sharing topics, including those listed under Topics for Partner Sharing starting on page 126, and those you come up with yourself. Mix and match the structures with topics. In time, you'll see which combinations best engage and stretch your class.

Assign Partners

Purposefully assign each student a partner for sharing. To create pairs, consider the social and academic skills students need to practice or stretch. For example, does the class need to build greater cohesiveness? Perhaps pairing students with classmates they don't usually interact with will help. Is the class in the middle of a research project? Pairing students who are researching similar topics can spark ideas and enthusiasm.

Inside-Outside Circles

Have students count off by twos. The ones form an inner circle and face out. The twos form an outer circle and face in, so pairs of students are now facing each other. Give students a topic to discuss, such as what they like studying in school and why. Allow students one minute to share with their partners. On your signal, the outside circle moves one person to the right while the inside circle stays in place, and everyone shares with a new partner. Repeat as many rounds as time allows.

As students become comfortable with this structure, you can change topics each time they change partners. You can also vary which circle moves and in which direction.

Maître d'

Tell students that you will pretend to be the maître d' in a restaurant and will call out groupings, such as "Tables for two" or "Tables for three." When you name a grouping, students form the specified groups. Once everyone is in a group, give them a topic to discuss (for example, favorite costume, prediction about what will happen in a read-aloud book, something they're looking forward to, ways they use math in everyday life). After a short time, ring a chime and call out a new grouping. Students regroup and you name a new topic to discuss.

Challenge students to form groups with classmates they don't usually talk with.

Mix and Mingle

To begin, students mix and mingle in the center of the circle. When you ring a chime, they pause and pair up with a student near them. Once everyone has a partner, give them a topic to discuss (for example, favorite holiday tradition, how they are similar to or different from the main character in a book they're reading, what they found most interesting in yesterday's discussion of World War II). After a minute or two, ring the chime again and students once again mix and mingle until you signal that it's time to find a new partner. Continue through several rounds.

Challenge students to pair up with people who are not their usual partners or best friends. Topics can be either social or academic.

Pair Up With a Neighbor

Students simply pair up with the person to their right or left in the circle. Partners take turns talking about the chosen topic. After a few minutes, if time and students' skills permit, you might invite a few students to tell the whole class something their partner said.

Topics for Partner Sharing

Character Connection

Students pair up and chat briefly about a book character they connect with. Provide a structure for the partner chat. Each person will 1) name the book they're reading, 2) name the character, and 3) say how the character connects to their life. Model the sharing: "I read *Freak the Mighty* by Rodman Philbrick. I connected with Max because his friends are very important to him, just like mine are to me. He walked over ten miles to the hospital to see his sick friend when no one would drive him there." Before students begin, remind them about appropriate voice level when half the class is talking simultaneously.

This could also be done as an around-the-circle or focused-topic dialogue sharing.

My Partner's Future

Assign partners and then tell students that they will each name a career they're interested in and why. For example: "I want to be a veterinarian because I love all kinds of animals" or "I want to be an author because I love to read and write stories." After students talk together, they'll summarize for the whole class what their partners said.

VARIATION ▪ Younger students can talk about "what I want to be when I grow up."

What We Have in Common

Pair students with someone they don't usually work or play with. Partners will chat for about two minutes with a goal of discovering two things they have in common. Challenge them to go beyond the obvious (for example, both are wearing jeans). To help students meet this challenge, you could brainstorm with them beforehand to generate a list of questions that will help them discover commonalities.

At a signal, students stop their conversation and together plan and practice how they'll share one of their commonalities with the whole class. When all are ready, go around the circle and have each pair name one commonality.

VARIATION ▪ When doing this variation, plan for a shorter greeting and group activity (or use this as a combined sharing and group activity). In advance, make copies of blank Venn diagrams for students to fill out with partners. Pairs then find out not only what they have in common but also a few things that are unique to each of them. With a student volunteer, model the conversation (for example, discuss books, music, family members, and favorites) and also demonstrate how to fill out the Venn diagram as you talk. If time permits, ask each pair to share with the class one thing they have in common. You may also want to collect the completed Venn diagrams for later use.

Dialogue Sharing

Structures to Support Success

The following two structures set students up for success with dialogue sharing. Both can be used for either open- or focused-topic dialogue sharing.

Sharing Jar

This structure helps students learn to state a main idea and supporting details. Place in front of you an empty container, a lid for the container, and five items in three different colors (for example, one green item for the main idea, three yellow items for supporting details, one red item for a concluding statement). For younger students, you could use counting bears; for older students, you might use tiles, cubes, or marbles.

Introduce and model the sharing. For example:

- "On the weekends, I enjoy scrapbooking." (Put the green item in the container.)
- "I love to look through my photos and decide how to put them in my scrapbook." (Put a yellow item in the container.)

- "Then I find some stickers to go with my photos." (Put another yellow item in the container.)
- "Finally, I write a fun caption for each photo." (Put a third yellow item in the container.)
- "I feel proud when I've finished a scrapbook page." (Put the red item in the container and place the lid on the jar.)

Continue to use the sharing jar until students become more comfortable with the main-idea-and-supporting-details structure.

Who Can Name One Thing I Said?

This structure helps students focus on the specifics in a classmate's sharing. Let students know that as the sharer speaks, their job is to listen carefully and remember key details. Sharers state a main idea and several supporting details and then ask, "Who can remember one thing I said?" They then call on students one at a time to state just one detail until all key details have been recalled.

VARIATION FOR YOUNGER CHILDREN ▪ Sharers hold up a photo or drawing (of a family pet, for example) and say three things about it. They then ask, "Who can name one thing I said?" and call on up to three people to respond.

Topics for Dialogue Sharing

Take a Walk

A day or two before doing this focused-topic sharing, take students on a walk to find an object to bring back to class (or ask them to bring in an object from home). Tell them the rules for these objects: They must be safe, OK to take, and small enough to fit in their hand. You may also want to have a few objects handy, such as various leaves and rocks, in case students forget theirs.

To show students how to succinctly share a main idea and a couple of supporting details, model the sharing first. For example: "I chose this stick because it still has an acorn on it. This makes me think of the oak tree in my back yard. I love all the leaves that come off that tree in the fall. We rake a huge pile of leaves and jump in them for hours."

Then call on the day's sharers. Spread this out over several days so that all students get a chance to talk about the object they found.

Tomorrow's Technology

This focused topic connects well to science learning. In advance (perhaps during the previous day's science class), challenge students to think about items they use and ways to make them better (for example, a lunchbox that keeps food cold far longer than the typical lunchbox). To emphasize the science connection, introduce the sharing by saying, "Scientists and engineers think about how to improve things so that they use less energy, cost less to make, and so on. Beginning today, each of you will have a chance to share an idea for making something you use even better."

Model for students: "Something I use a lot is hand lotion. I would like to design a device that goes in the lotion bottle and makes sure you can get all the lotion out. I always feel I waste so much because I can't get all of it out." As students share, you could record their ideas for use in another lesson.

Group Activity

A fifth grade class is intent on guessing a category made up by their classmate, Caleb, who is doling out indirect clues in a game called Aunt Minerva (page 155).

"Aunt Minerva likes Florida but doesn't like Alaska," announces Caleb.

No responses.

Caleb tries again. "Aunt Minerva likes heavy down quilts but doesn't like thin sheets."

Two hands shoot up and Caleb calls on Sonya.

"Aunt Minerva likes soup but doesn't like ice cream?" ventures Sonya, her voice making the statement a question.

"That's true," nods Caleb. "Danny?"

Danny has retracted his hand after hearing Sonya's contribution. "Nope, I'm not ready yet."

After a few more guesses about Aunt Minerva's preferences, half the hands in the circle are raised, and Mr. Bergstrom, the teacher, spots a good stopping place. All have grappled with the process of set-making that's integral to this

131

game and Mr. Bergstrom knows it's important to stop while students are still engaged with the activity.

"Pick a guesser, Caleb," Mr. Bergstrom directs, and Caleb points to Josie.

"Is it hot and cold?" she asks.

Caleb's smile and nod confirm it.

Meanwhile, down the hall a sixth grade class is playing Beachball Math (page 156) to practice finding the least common multiple of two numbers, something the class is working on. Most students figure out their answer with relative ease; a few lean to a neighbor for help.

And on the first floor, in a second grade classroom a chorus of seven- and eight-year-old voices offers up a singsong rendition of the October stanza from Maurice Sendak's (1962) poem "Chicken Soup with Rice."

> In October
> I'll be host
> to witches, goblins
> and a ghost.
> I'll serve them
> chicken soup
> on toast.
> Whoopy once
> whoopy twice
> whoopy chicken soup
> with rice.

"We've got the words down," says their teacher, "and now we're going to do it in our scary voices. Take a minute and think about how you can make your voice sound scary."

Eyes twinkle as the children await their teacher's signal to begin. In a dramatic transformation from their earlier version, the young voices have grown deep and mysterious or high and quavery. As they finish, they break into grins and delighted laughter, reveling in the sound of their collectively expressive voices.

Their teacher offers a compliment. "Mmm . . . very nice. Let's think about reciting that at next week's All-School Meeting."

PURPOSES AND REFLECTIONS

As the above vignettes illustrate, group activities are short and fast-paced, and involve everyone in the class. Though they may appear to be "just for fun," they support crucial learning goals: Some activities incorporate academic skill-building components that tie in to current topics in the curriculum; others offer practice in important generalized skills like listening, following directions, exercising self-control, or practicing deductive reasoning; still others help build a positive classroom community.

Purposes of Group Activity

- Contributes to the class's sense of community and group identity by building a repertoire of common songs, games, chants, and poems

- Fosters active and engaged participation

- Encourages inclusion and cooperation

- Can help students learn the value of persistence and practice

- Strengthens academic and social skills

Group activity contributes to the class's sense of community and group identity

It's cleanup time and Shawna and Leo are methodically taking the large wooden unit blocks from their skyscraper and stacking them neatly on the appointed shelf. "Whoopy once, whoopy twice," chants Leo under his breath as he leans from the pile of blocks to the shelf, lost in his rhythm of stack and tidy and lean. "Whoopy chicken soup with rice," Shawna chimes in. Her voice layers over her companion's as neatly as the blocks they stack on the shelf.

The chants and songs, games and story lines introduced during group activity time are a common and important currency in the learning community. They contribute to a shared archive from which students can draw whether it's during a companionable cleanup moment, on a field trip bus ride, or at the lunch table. We feel a sense of belonging, comfort, and acceptance when we recognize a familiar melody, when we are invited into a game and realize that we know the rules, when someone refers to a funny story and we find that we know that story, too. We are at home in this place, with these people.

Sometimes the common learning gives us a way to affirm our group identity within a larger community. When the second grade stands before the rest of the school and intones their ghosts-and-goblins stanza of "Chicken Soup with Rice" as a cohesive group, it's a wonderful declaration of their solidarity.

Group activity fosters active and engaged participation

Good choices for group activities are engaging rather than passive and require everyone's participation. They can be a great "wake-up call" at the start of the day because they demand that each of us pays attention and contributes. It's not easy to snooze through a fast-paced game of Zoom (page 167). And you need to pay attention when your turn to think up an equation for today's date is coming soon and the first six people have used up the obvious number statements.

Joining the tempo of a well-chosen group activity can help students find a productive pace for moving into the rest of the day. As individuals, we all have different rhythms and gaits, and our differences bring richness to the group. We also have days when our pace is "off." Students may come to school distracted, replaying a breakfast table argument with a sibling. Or they may arrive frazzled, rushing to compensate for oversleeping, needing help to change gears and settle down. Joining a group activity, moving in unison, enables students to focus and find a comfortable stride.

Whether boisterous or calm, playful or serious, group activities are short and fast-paced, and involve everyone in the class.

Group activity encourages inclusion and cooperation

Good group activities allow all members to take part. Although some students will excel in certain activities and some in others, each group activity must be accessible to all and allow everyone to begin the day with a sense of success. A teacher's knowledge of her class will guide the choice of activities. They shouldn't all feel easy—a sure route to complaints of "boring." But neither should they be ones in which only a couple of "gifted" students can feel successful; that will demoralize and isolate the rest of the group. Celebrating individual talents and achievements is healthy in a classroom, but group activity is not the place for it.

Group activities should be cooperative, not competitive, in nature. If you occasionally want to introduce an element of competition, try having the group "compete" against itself. Can they beat their previous time at Telegraph (page 166), a game in which they must work together to pass a hand squeeze around the circle as quickly as possible? Can they come up with more equations that equal 23 on the 23rd of this month than they could on the 23rd of last month? Many classes enjoy keeping a log of their best times for various activities. But even this kind of competition is best used sparingly, so that the emphasis remains on the activity rather than the contest.

Group activity can help students learn the value of persistence and practice

Successful activities can stretch the group in positive ways. Helping the class to notice their increasing proficiency with a challenging activity affirms the role of practice and persistence in learning. But the challenges need to be deliberate choices on the teacher's part. He must first be sure that a sufficient level of safety has developed within the group, and then choose activities that highlight the whole group's growth, rather than that of individuals.

I once heard a group of fifth graders groan, upon a first read-through of the Gettysburg Address during social studies, "We'll never be able to say this! We can't even pronounce half these words." And they were right. They couldn't pronounce them. Over the following two weeks, the class used Morning Meeting time to supplement their learning of the speech. During group activity, the teacher coached and students practiced. At the end of those two weeks, these fifth graders could do more than pronounce. They proclaimed—with resonant voices and not a single stumble.

"Remember how two weeks ago you thought you were never going to be able to recite this?" their teacher reminded them. This is such an important lesson: that what seems insurmountable at first can indeed be surmounted with effort and support. Learning this lesson will serve these students well as they go on to confront the mysteries of algebra or the unfamiliar constructions of a new language.

Group activity strengthens academic and social skills

Group activity abounds with opportunities to integrate the academic curriculum. In addition, because the activities are interactive, they also teach and reinforce social skills. However, to ensure that all students start their day with a sense of accomplishment and a reminder that they are successful learners, Morning Meeting group activities are designed to enable students to practice, apply, or extend familiar skills and concepts. The introduction of new material is best saved for specific instructional periods.

Many games lend themselves to the incorporation of academic material such as content area vocabulary or math skills practice. Even when games don't directly incorporate curriculum content, they teach skills that are important to academic success: observing, focusing, collaborating, thinking creatively, problem-solving.

And group activities don't have to be games. A successful activity might be a group recitation of a poem, as in this chapter's opening vignette. It might be a round of group story-writing, with an emphasis on trying varied sentence structures, or a chant with repeating phrases that reinforce pattern recognition. All these pursuits can be highly engaging for students while strengthening their academic and social skills.

Highlights of Group Activity

- Provides a way for all class members to learn a common set of songs, chants, games, and poems
- Allows the group to experience working together to produce an outcome impossible as individuals or a small group
- Encourages cooperation and inclusion
- Reinforces and extends academic and social-emotional skills
- Allows the integration of curriculum content
- Fosters active and engaged participation
- Allows students to see one another's unique strengths
- Provides the experience of having fun together as a group

You may want to browse through Group Activities to Try starting on page 152 before continuing.

GETTING STARTED

Model appropriate behaviors when introducing group activity

Just as with all classroom activities, how a teacher introduces Morning Meeting group activity has a big impact on students' success with it. Explain that this is a time within Morning Meeting when the whole group will do an activity together. In whatever language is appropriate and respectful to the age group, note that it will be important in these activities for each person to take good care of herself or himself, as well as taking care of other people in the group. I've found it works well to begin by saying something like, "The third part of our Morning Meeting each day will be doing an activity together as a whole group. We'll be moving, talking, acting, singing, chanting, or playing a game. As we do all these active things, what will we need to remember to do so that all of us can enjoy this time and learn together?"

After students share some ideas, choose a couple that are important to the activity for the day and model constructive behaviors related to those ideas. Eventually, you'll find it helpful to model the following:

- How to move safely through the circle
- How to keep your body in control
- How to wait for your turn
- What to do if someone makes a mistake
- What voice level to use (for speaking, chanting, and singing)
- What to do if a classmate needs help
- How to help everyone feel included
- How to work with a partner or small group

"Eventually" is a key word here. Opportunities to model activities and discuss how they're going will happen throughout the year. Carefully choose relatively simple, low-risk activities at the outset so that the group experiences success

Teachers choose relatively simple, low-risk activities at the outset so that the group experiences success without the need for extensive preparation.

without the need for extensive preparation. Modeling one element at a time, specifically and thoroughly, works better than trying to conduct an exhaustive Grand Tour of constructive activity behaviors.

Also, spend some time thinking about what academic skills the class might need to learn or review for a group activity you're planning, and then teach the skills one at a time so students have a scaffold for achieving success. As the class is ready, you can add variations to the activity or introduce new, more complex activities.

For younger children, consider teaching complex activities over several days. For example, for songs, chants, and poems, start by having children simply echo each line as you read it. On another day, have the class sing or recite the lines chorally without echoing you. Still later, add movements for each line.

For older students, you can often similarly break down complex activities but cover all the steps in the same meeting. For example, the first time students do What Are You Doing? (page 166), a pantomime activity in which two students at a time interact in the center of the circle, you might model how to move safely into and out of the center, how to do the pantomime, and how to interact respectfully.

Interactive Modeling (see pages 26–27 in the Overview chapter) is an effective way to teach or review skills students need for a group activity. "Today we're going to play a fast and in-control game of Speed Ball" (page 165), Mr. Coughlin tells his first grade class. "I'm going to throw the ball to Willy. Watch and tell me what makes my throw both fast and in control." He throws the ball low and carefully and Willy catches it easily.

"What did you notice that made that throw both fast and in control?"

"You didn't wing it at him," volunteers Zeke.

"That's right. And where did I aim it?"

"At his belly."

Mr. Coughlin nods.

"You threw it kind of easy," offers Claire.

"Why did I do that? Wouldn't it be faster to throw it hard?"

"No," maintains Claire. "Because Willy's not that far away from you and it would probably just bounce off him, or it would go out of the circle and he would have to go get it and then it would really slow things down."

Aaron's hand is up. He is a versatile and talented athlete and loves any chance to throw a ball—or talk about it. "If you were throwing at Amy or somebody all the way across the circle, you'd have to throw harder, though."

"So you noticed," summarizes Mr. Coughlin, naming specific behaviors with key words that can be quick reminders later, "that I used careful aim and a just-hard-enough throw, depending on whom I'm throwing to."

He then invites a student volunteer to demonstrate a throw using those behaviors. Finally, Mr. Coughlin has the class practice briefly before beginning the Speed Ball activity "for real." The modeling takes only a few minutes, and Mr. Coughlin offers a chance for students to try applying the behaviors right away—an important step in helping students truly absorb new learning.

Model how to handle mistakes

Fourth grade teacher Mr. Roth is determined that his classroom will be one in which making a mistake is fine for any student—during group activity or any other time of day. He conveys this message daily in various ways, from displaying a poster on the wall that says "The only person who doesn't make a mistake is a person who never does anything" to telling stories from his own everyday life that feature an error in thinking and the learning he gained from it. It is not a message accepted readily by nine-year-olds, who are painfully aware and critical of their own and their peers' imperfections, so when Mr. Roth introduces a new group activity in which students create equations, he uses modeling to help them learn how to respond when mistakes are made.

"When we do an activity like this, we will sometimes make mistakes," he says. "It's important that we notice mistakes in an honest and respectful way so that we can learn from them."

Earlier he had enlisted Jocelyn, a student for whom math comes easily, to help with today's modeling. Now he brings her into the lesson: "Today is the fourth. Jocelyn, please make up an equation using the number four that has a mistake in it. I'm going to be a student who catches the mistake. Everyone, watch me and notice how I respond."

"One hundred divided by twenty is four," offers Jocelyn, writing it on the chart.

Mr. Roth looks thoughtful for a moment and then slowly puts his hand up. "I think that one hundred divided by twenty is five."

Breaking out of acting mode, he turns to the class and asks, "What did you notice?"

Kelly responds first: "You didn't shoot your hand up really fast, like, 'Ooh, ooh, I see a mistake!'"

"What did I do?" asks Mr. Roth.

Group Activity

"You put it up like normal—it wasn't a big deal," Kelly adds, and other students chime in.

"You kept your voice nice and didn't sound know-it-all."

"You said what you thought was right, not that Jocelyn was wrong."

"You didn't laugh or roll your eyes."

"What did my face look like?" inquires Mr. Roth.

"You had your regular face on."

As the modeling ends and flows seamlessly into the activity, Mr. Roth watches for students putting their newly learned skill into action when classmates make mistakes.

Reflecting on the lesson later, he's pleased that the students recognized the details of what makes for an honest and respectful response to a mistake. He also knows that habits don't change easily and that in the days and weeks ahead, eyes will roll and hands will wave excitedly at a mistake. And he will remind, redirect, and reinforce—always with the same respect he has asked students to show when they notice others' mistakes.

Choose activities that fit the group at this particular time

Group activities can vary widely. Some involve movement, others are more stationary; some are playful, others serious; many draw on the curriculum; some are brainteasers, while others tap students' artistic side. Choosing activities highlights the teacher's role as balance-keeper and knower-of-the-group. Students' maturity levels, their experience with doing group activities, their academic and social skill levels, the season of the school year, the group's degree of cohesiveness and its temperament are all factors in determining which activities will be most beneficial.

Is it the beginning of the year, before students even know each other's names? If so, naming, introduction, or interview activities tend to work well. Mid-year, when

*The teacher chooses activities that fit the class's maturity
level, the academic and social skills they're working on,
and the group's temperment.*

the class has begun to build trust and is developing a repertoire of academic and social skills, you might choose more complex or curriculum-based activities.

Is this a group of serious eighth graders who could use some lightening up? Perhaps Zoom (page 167) or Zip, Zap, Pop (page 167) would be just the thing. Or do you have a class of fourth graders who lack confidence in academics? Memorizing a serious and beautiful poem together may help them look at themselves differently.

In upper grades, when students are going through rapid physical and emotional changes, you will want to pay particular attention to students' developmental needs. A sixth or seventh grader who is very conscious of leaving childhood behind and eager to be considered more adult might benefit from an activity such as Pica Fermé Nada (page 164), which requires increased skill and self-control. But a fifth grader might be delighted to engage in a familiar childhood game like Coseeki/Follow the Leader (page 158), and an eighth grader might relish the same game for the opportunity to regress for a few minutes.

Keep in mind that throughout the year you can adjust any activity to meet the developmental needs, abilities, and mood of the students you're teaching to best support their learning and growth. As you look at a particular activity, consider how you might adapt it to incorporate aspects of your specific academic curriculum. Also ask yourself how you might adapt it to accommodate a group that is:

- Shy, nervous, or reluctant to participate
- Rowdy and silly
- Still gaining all the knowledge and skills needed to participate successfully

Finally, consider shifting to students some of the responsibility for making activities work. Many teachers, after introducing a new activity, ask the group some reflective questions:

1. What made it work?
2. What made it engaging?
3. What could we do next time to make it even more successful?

This gets students thinking about how they work together and increases their investment.

Look to academics for activity ideas

Keep in mind that coming up with group activity ideas needn't be one more thing to add on to your busy day; instead, they can spring from the content you're already teaching.

Picture these scenes. A group of seventh graders, totally involved, mentally wrestle together with a tricky logic problem drawn from their math unit. Down the hall, third graders clap out the syllables in their weekly list of spelling words, feet tapping along. In a first grade room, the class is proudly reading in unison a poem hand-lettered in large print on an easel in the circle. In another primary class, students are using their bodies to make a beaver lodge and act out the activities of a beaver colony, representing and extending the learning they have gained from their study of beavers.

Each of these activities comes straight from the class's curricula, and meets the criteria for group activity perfectly: They are noncompetitive and inclusive; they require attention and alertness; they build the group's sense of how they can problem-solve together; they develop a group voice, intelligence, and identity.

When you're looking for activity ideas, think about your curriculum. Could students work through some math problems together? Play a word game that will build vocabulary? Construct a crossword puzzle that they post on the school website? Could you find a poem about rivers that would tie in to the week's geography focus and make a great choral reading?

Upper grades teachers could get ideas for curriculum-based activities from cross-discipline colleagues. A language arts teacher might have a great word game that she could teach the math and science teachers and vice versa. Weekly team meetings can provide a good venue for sharing ideas.

Group Activity

Group activity time might also be the perfect opportunity for a structured discussion. Have students form two circles, one inside the other, with the inside circle turned outward so each student is facing a partner. Pose an open-ended question (one that has many possible reasonable answers) drawn from the curriculum—perhaps "Why do you think the protagonist in our story went against the wishes of his team?" or "Which historical figure from the civil rights movement would you like to meet and why?" Students share responses with their partners, and then, on your signal, take a step to the right and trade responses with a new partner (to the same question or a new one you pose). After several rounds, a few students share with the whole group what their partners said. Again, the activity is inclusive, enriching, and engaging, and it comes right out of the class's academic work.

A final word: As the discussion above makes clear, group activities—like the rest of school—need to be engaging, but they don't always have to be full of frivolity. Remind yourself that it's not your role as a teacher to be an entertainer, and that the best learning comes from engagement, which can take the form of deep

Group activities don't need to be full of frivolity. They do need to be engaging, which can take the form of deep concentration or fascination.

concentration, even fascination, as well as playfulness and laughter. So instead of focusing on making activities entertaining for students, use your knowledge of the group to choose activities that will engage them.

For a wide variety of group activities to help you get started, see Group Activities to Try on pages 152–167.

Group activity responsibilities

In implementing and assessing group activity, keep the following general responsibilities in mind.

Teachers' Responsibilities

- Choose a variety of age-appropriate activities that include all skill levels.

- Make sure many different kinds of activities are represented—songs, poems, games, chants, movement, etc.—and that children have a chance to be physical, intellectual, artistic, playful, and serious.

- Give directions that are simple, clear, and consistent.

- Make sure everyone knows the rules for each activity.

- Model and practice skills that children need to be successful.

- Select activities that are inclusive of all and cooperative rather than competitive in nature.

- Model being playful and enthusiastic without being silly.

- Stop the activity and regroup if it's not going well.

- Reflect with students when necessary to make the next group activity more successful.

Group Activity

Students' Responsibilities

- Participate fully in all activities.

- Interact with all classmates.

- Show respect and support for the efforts of all participants.

- Have fun without being silly.

- Keep bodies and voice level in control.

- Work hard without being competitive.

- Follow the rules of activities.

FINE TUNINGS

Q I have several ELL students in my classroom. What do I need to keep in mind as I plan group activities so that the activities are inclusive of them?

ANSWER ▪ Group activities offer ELL students many opportunities to practice language in a relaxed way. Early in the year, plan group activities that require simple language and offer physical or picture cues to support the use of English. As the year goes on, gradually increase the language complexity of activities. And always consider cultural comfort levels. For example, if a student's culture restricts physical contact with people outside the family, choose activities (especially at the start of the year) that do not involve touching classmates.

Often a simple variation in an activity can make it suitable for ELL students and the rest of the class. Here are some examples:

- *Beach Ball Vocabulary* (page 157), with the variation of placing a picture sticker instead of a vocabulary word in each section of the ball. Also, students can simply name the item pictured and use it in a sentence without giving a definition of the item.

- *Cooper Says* (page 158), with instructions that vary depending on the student's language goals. For example, "Stand behind the chair. Sit on the chair. Stand in front of the chair. Put your pencil on the chair."

- *Near and Far.* In this variation of Hot and Cold (page 160), classmates give the seeker distance clues, such as "You're getting nearer . . . you're very near it" or "You're far away" instead of "hot" and "cold," which, used in this manner, could confuse students beginning to learn English.

Q I know that activities should be engaging and enjoyable, but
my class gets really silly and doesn't take them seriously.
Any suggestions?

ANSWER ▪ You're right to draw a distinction between enjoying something and
being silly. Whereas enjoyment can enhance learning, silliness is distracting and
gets in the way of group engagement. Monitoring the tone is an important teacher
job in Morning Meeting. Give a reminder at the first sign of silliness, before that
tone takes hold.

Sometimes students need more than a reminder. Observe to see where the silliness is coming from. If it's one or two students, directing them to "take a break"
(go to positive time-out) often works to stop the behavior and keep the silliness
from spreading. Also consider whether something about the particular activity
is making it hard for those students to join in wholeheartedly. You may need to
speak to them individually to say what you notice and ask them to think of ways
they can help group activity work better.

When the silliness is group-wide, I have called a class time-out and then led the
group in reflecting on what is going on so we can come up with possible solutions.
Maybe a change in the activities themselves is in order. Perhaps it's time to switch
for a while to very structured activities that offer greater challenge and help the
group take itself more seriously.

The bottom line is that you shouldn't be afraid to stop an activity that feels too silly
so you can take corrective action. And remember the importance of responding immediately, when the behavior is still minor, to keep things from getting out of hand.

Q The same students always seem to "star" in group activity.
How can I address this?

ANSWER ▪ One important way is to make sure the activities are varied, calling
upon many different modes of communication and interaction. We all have different areas in which we shine and in which we struggle. Some of us are graceful

**Group
Activity**

In time, students learn they can participate even
if they don't excel at the activity of the moment.

and coordinated; some are verbally quick and playful. Some have terrific recall and excel at memory games and recitation; others are theatrical and can pantomime any emotion down to its every nuance. Still others have a gift of melody that enables a class to sound beautiful when they sing together.

Making sure our activities engage many different aptitudes ensures that all students will have a chance to shine—and not shine. Anyone may sometimes feel a little foolish; all will often feel smart. In time, students learn they can participate even if they don't excel at the activity of the moment. Marisol learns that when she stands next to Casey she can, in fact, carry a tune. Wesley learns that if he forgets a line in the skit, he can glance at Habiba, who will remember and give him a cue.

Q **One of the students in this year's class hangs back and is very reluctant to participate in group activity. How can I encourage this child to join in?**

ANSWER ▪ This is a situation in which a teacher's knowledge of individual students is crucial. What does this student choose to do at recess or choice times? What are his or her areas of comfort and skill? Suppose the student is like Giselle, who excels at anything with the suffix "-ball." Then you could choose some activities involving ball-throwing. If the student is like Steven, who has a wealth of information about the latest world conflict or most recent movie blockbuster, you could structure some activities around current events.

Another possibility with a shy or reticent student: If you're teaching the group a new activity, you might elicit this student's help ahead of time to try it out and co-teach it to the group with you.

Group Activity

GROUP ACTIVITIES TO TRY

Group Activity	Beginning of Year	Later in Year	Younger Grades	Older Grades	Song, Chant, Movement	Academic Content Reinforcement
✶ Alibi, p. 154		●		●		
✶ Alphabet Story, p. 154		●	●	●		●
Aroostasha, p. 154	●		●	●	●	
Aunt Minerva, p. 155		●		●		●
A Warm Wind Blows, p. 156	●		●	●		
Beach Ball Activities, p. 156		●	●	●		●
Category Snap, p. 157		●	●	●	●	●
Clapping Names, p. 158	●		●		●	
Cooper Says, p. 158	●		●	●		
✶ Coseeki/Follow the Leader, p. 158	●		●	●		
Famous Pairs, p. 159		●		●		●
Guess the Number, p. 159		●	●	●		●
Hands Up for '14, p. 160		●		●	●	●
Hot and Cold, p. 160	●		●	●		
Human Protractor, p. 161		●	●	●		●
✶ Incorporations, p. 161		●	●	●		

Group Activity	Beginning of Year	Later in Year	Younger Grades	Older Grades	Song, Chant, Movement	Academic Content Reinforcement
Mental Math Pushups, p. 162		●		●		●
My Bonny, p. 162	●		●		●	
Mystery Word, p. 162		●	●	●		●
Nonverbal Birthday Lineup, p. 163	●			●		
Oliver Twist, p. 163	●		●		●	
One Thing You Like to Do, p. 164	●		●	●	●	
Pica Fermé Nada, p. 164		●		●		●
Scientific Pros and Cons, p. 165		●		●		●
Speed Ball, p. 165		●	●	●		
Take Sides, p. 166	●		●	●		
Telegraph, p. 166		●	●	●		
What Are You Doing? p. 166		●	●	●	●	
Zip, Zap, Pop, p. 167		●	●	●		
Zoom, p. 167		●	●	●		

Group Activities to Try

Alibi

Choose a student to be the detective and have her leave the room. While she is out, the group chooses one person to be the gremlin and another to be the spokesperson. The gremlin changes something obvious in the room, such as moving the hamster's cage. All students act as suspects and make up one-sentence alibis (for example, "I never moved from this spot!").

When the detective returns to the circle, the spokesperson tells her what has changed. Going around the circle, the detective asks each student, "Where were you when [the hamster's cage was moved]?" Students state their alibis.

The detective now goes around the circle a second time, again asking for alibis. Everyone but the gremlin restates their original alibi—the gremlin changes his alibi slightly. The detective then has three guesses to discover the gremlin. If she doesn't guess correctly, the gremlin says, "I did it!"

VARIATION ▪ To make this more challenging, students could add more details to their alibis or all students except the gremlin could change their alibis.

Alphabet Story

The first person in the circle starts telling a story with a sentence beginning with the letter "A": "Aunt Helen came to my house the other day." The next person in the circle continues, adding a sentence that begins with "B": "Buddy, her terrier, came with her." The class continues through the alphabet until everyone has added to the story.

Aroostasha

Students stand in a circle with their hands clasped in front of them, fingers interlaced. Begin the activity by demonstrating the chant and body movements. Chant "Aroostasha, aroostasha, aroostasha-sha" while moving your clasped hands from the right side of your body to the left and pulsing your hands up and down to the beat. Then do the chant while moving your hands back to the right side of your body, pulsing to the beat as you go. Have the class repeat the chant and body movements after you.

Call out "thumbs up"; then chant and do the above movement with hands clasped and thumbs up. Call out "thumbs up, wrists together," and do the chant and movement with hands clasped, thumbs up, and wrists together.

Keep going in this way, adding one body position at a time. For example, you can add:

- Elbows in

- Knees together

- Toes in

- Bottom out

- Tongue out (Ever try to say "Aroostasha" with your tongue out? Kids really get a laugh out of this!)

Aunt Minerva

The student who starts the activity decides on a category but doesn't tell anyone. Instead, he hints at the category by naming things that Aunt Minerva likes and doesn't like. For example, if the category is "hot and cold" he might say, "Aunt Minerva likes Florida but doesn't like Alaska. Aunt Minerva likes heavy down quilts but doesn't like thin sheets." The other students try to figure out the category based on the clues. When a student thinks she knows the category, she gives an example of her own, without naming the category: "Aunt Minerva likes soup but doesn't like ice cream." The starter acknowledges whether the statement is true, and continues giving examples to help more classmates figure out the category.

To avoid the scenario of the class waiting for the last few students to catch on, have the starter reveal the category when a solid number of classmates have guessed it. Then choose another student to begin a new round.

A Warm Wind Blows

Bring chairs into the meeting circle—the number of chairs should be one less than the number of people in the circle. Everyone sits except for one student, who stands in the middle of the circle. He says, "A warm wind blows for anyone who _____" filling in the blank with a category (for example, "has a dog"). Everyone who fits that category comes into the center of the circle and then quickly finds a new place to sit, including the student who started in the middle. The one person who doesn't find a seat now stands in the center of the circle and says, "A warm wind blows for anyone who _____," naming a new category. The activity continues for several rounds.

Encourage students to name categories that relate to interests, hobbies, and family rather than clothing or appearance. You could brainstorm a list of categories before beginning the activity.

Beach Ball Activities

You can use multi-paneled beach balls in a number of activities that reinforce academic skills. Instructions here are for math and language arts, but you can adapt the activity for many subject areas.

Beach Ball Math

Before doing the activity, write a number on each panel of a beach ball and the small circles at the top and bottom of the ball.

Begin by announcing a math function, such as addition, subtraction, multiplication, or division and then tossing the ball to someone in the circle. The person who catches the ball looks at the numbers beneath or near her hands. These numbers become an equation that the student tries to solve using the designated function. For example, if the function is multiplication and the student's hands cover a three and a seven, she needs to multiply three times seven and give the correct answer. The student can ask for help if needed. Once the equation is solved, the student tosses the ball to someone else in the group.

Beach Ball Vocabulary

Instead of numbers, write vocabulary words on each panel of a beach ball. The student who catches the ball defines one of the words near where his hands are and uses it in a sentence.

If you have students who are struggling readers or just learning English, you can vary this activity by placing picture stickers on each panel. The student who catches the ball looks at the stickers under or near her hands. She names one of the items and then uses that word in a sentence.

Category Snap

The group sits in a circle. The leader starts a rhythm using a sequence of knee slap, hand clap, right-hand finger snap, left-hand finger snap. Once the rhythm is established, he announces a category, such as fruits, on the right-hand finger snap and names an example, such as apples, with the left-hand finger snap. The next person in the circle repeats "apples" with the right-hand finger snap and then a new example in that same category with the left-hand finger snap: Knee slap, hand clap, "apples, apricots." The play continues around the circle. Once an item has been named, it cannot be used again.

VARIATION ■ Announce the category before the activity begins. Give students a moment to think of several examples of that category, and let students know that they'll need to pay attention and remember what each classmate says. Then, going around the circle, each person names an item—with no repetitions.

Once everyone has named an item, the leader begins the knee slap, hand clap, finger snap rhythm. With the right-hand finger snap, she names her own item and with the left-hand finger snap she names another student's item. That student then names his own item and another student's item and so on. This variation sends the action jumping around the circle.

Clapping Names

Children clap out the number of syllables in each child's first name while they chant the name. You can begin with your own name; then either go around the room or ask children to volunteer to be next. You can vary the activity by

having children clap out last names or self-chosen nicknames.

This is a good activity to do at the beginning of the year when children are learning each other's names. It's also good to do if a new child joins the class later in the year.

Cooper Says

This activity is similar to "Simon Says," except that no one is ever "out." The leader, "Cooper," gives the group instructions. Students follow the instructions only if the instructions are preceded by "Cooper says . . ." For example, if the leader says, "Cooper says touch your toes," students touch their toes. However, if the leader says, "Touch your toes," students stand still. Keep the activity moving quickly. You can increase the difficulty by challenging the group to follow ten directions correctly.

Coseeki/Follow the Leader

One student leaves the circle and stands where she cannot see the group. The group chooses a leader who does a movement, such as tapping his toe, which the others follow. The leader changes the movement regularly and the others follow his movement. The hidden student returns, stands in the middle of the circle, watches the movements, and tries to guess who the leader is. If she doesn't guess correctly after three tries, reveal the leader to limit frustration and keep the activity positive.

- Have more than one guesser and have them confer before guessing.

- Have two leaders take turns starting new movements. The guesser tries to identify both leaders.

- Use movements that make no sound.

Famous Pairs

Make a list of famous pairs of people with whom the class is familiar, such as Lewis and Clark or Abbott and Costello. You could brainstorm a list with the class. Write these names on cards, one name to a card, and then tape a card to each student's back. Students mill around, asking each other questions to determine what name is on their back. They then find the person who has their partner's name. Pairs return to the circle, standing or sitting next to each other.

Guess the Number

Tell the class you've chosen a number between one and _____, naming a range that's appropriately challenging for the age and skill level of the group. Going around the circle, students ask yes-or-no questions to try to determine the number (or say "pass" if they'd like). Anyone can try to guess the number at any time. If the guess is incorrect, the questioning continues.

If the guess is correct, start another round by choosing or having a student choose another number. To emphasize collaboration rather than competition, be sure the new number chooser isn't the person who guessed correctly in the previous round.

Encourage students to think of questions that will give them information about the number, rather than questions that just eliminate one number. For example, instead of asking if it's the number after fourteen, students might ask if it's a two-digit number, whether it's greater than ten, or if it has a five in it.

Group Activities to Try

Hands Up for '14

Name an academic category (for example, "capital cities") and choose a student to go first in naming something in that category. The group begins the following chant, filling in the name of the category in line four. The last line of the chant names the person who goes first. He says an item in the category; then, going quickly around the circle, each person names a different item in the category.

Chant:

> Hands up / / (silent beats)
>
> For '14 [change for correct year] / / (silent beats)
>
> Gonna name (clap, clap)
>
> Some [category] (clap, clap)
>
> One apiece (clap, clap)
>
> No repeats (clap, clap)
>
> No hesitation (clap, clap)
>
> No duplication (clap, clap)
>
> Starting with (clap, clap) [student's name]

Hot and Cold

Select an object to hide. Choose one student to be the "seeker" and send her out of the room. Hide the object in a place that is difficult enough to provide a challenge but not so difficult that the search becomes frustrating. The group can help you choose a good hiding place. Invite the seeker back into the room. The seeker begins looking for the object. The group guides the search by saying "hot" whenever the seeker gets near the object and "cold" whenever she moves away from the object.

VARIATION ▪ If you have ELL students in the class who might be confused by using "hot" and "cold" in this way, you can use "near" and "far."

Human Protractor

Everyone stands in a circle, hands touching toes. Tell students they're going to straighten up gradually, keeping their arms stretched out in front of their bodies. At the same time, they'll be counting from zero to a number that you specify. By the time their hands are reaching overhead, they should be at the upper number. Let students know that they need to remember where their hands are at different numbers, and set the range of numbers to suit the age and abilities in your classroom (0–10, 0–100, 0–180, and so on).

Once students have moved through the range of numbers from toes to overhead, call out numbers within the specified range. Students take the position for each number as you call it. When students are familiar with the activity, they can take turns being the number caller.

VARIATIONS

- Students count from 0 to 100 percent as they move from touching toes to reaching overhead. Then, instead of calling out numbers, you could ask probability questions, such as "What is the likelihood of rain today?"

- After students have moved through the number positions, have them do multiplication, addition, or subtraction problems that lead to an answer within the designated range. Each student does the calculation and then moves into the position for the answer. For example, if you called out "Three times fifteen" they'd take the position for 45.

⭐ Incorporations

At a signal from you, students will form and re-form groups as quickly as possible. Begin by ringing a chime or a bell and then give directions for forming groups, such as "Get into groups of three." Once the students have formed groups of three, ring the chime again and give a different direction, such as "Get into groups where everyone is wearing something the same color." This activity moves very quickly.

Mental Math Pushups

Write a series of math expressions on a whiteboard or chart (for example, $2 + 2 + 2$, $3 + 3 - 3$, $5 + 5 - 1$). Students work with a partner to find the answer to each expression in their head—no pencil or paper. When you give the signal, all students give their answers at the same time. To help students focus, begin by covering up all the expressions except the first one. Then uncover one expression at a time as the rounds continue.

My Bonny

Everyone sings the song "My Bonny Lies Over the Ocean." Whenever words beginning with a "b" are sung, students alternate between sitting and standing. For example: "My Bonny [stand] lies over the ocean. My Bonny [sit] lies over the sea . . ."

Words:

> My **B**onny lies over the ocean.
>
> My **B**onny lies over the sea.
>
> My **B**onny lies over the ocean,
>
> Oh **b**ring **b**ack my **B**onny to me.
>
> **B**ring **b**ack, **b**ring **b**ack,
>
> Oh **b**ring **b**ack my **B**onny to me, to me.
>
> **B**ring **b**ack, **b**ring **b**ack,
>
> Oh **b**ring **b**ack my **B**onny to me.

Mystery Word

On cards, write key vocabulary words from an article or topic students have been studying, one word per card. Begin by having students quickly summarize that article or topic and confirm that everyone is familiar with all the words written on the cards.

Choose a student to be "It" and tape a word to her back. Her job is to guess the word using clues from classmates. She moves slowly around the inside of the circle, back turned to her classmates so that they can see the word. They offer clues in the form of sentences that could include that word. For example, if students are studying environmental issues and the word is "extinct," a clue might be, "If sea ice keeps melting, polar bears might become blank."

Nonverbal Birthday Lineup

Students line up according to their month and day of birth, without any talking. This challenges students to be inventive in communicating nonverbally. Remind children that they need to remain friendly and respectful as they use facial expressions and body language to communicate.

Oliver Twist

The whole group chants the following song and does the accompanying movements. Begin slowly and then speed up until children are all laughing as they try to keep up.

Chant:

Oliver twist, twist, twist (hands on hips and twist body)

Can't do this, this, this (tap right foot and shake forefinger of right hand)

Touch his head, head, head (touch head with hands)

Touch his nose, nose, nose (touch nose with hands)

Touch his ears, ears, ears (touch ears with hands)

Touch his toes, toes, toes (touch toes)

One Thing You Like to Do

Let students know that they're each going to pantomime a favorite activity. Give them a minute to think of an activity and a simple movement they can do to represent that activity (for example, pretending to swing a baseball bat). Going around the circle, each student does his or her movement and classmates guess the activity. Remind students to wait until the pantomime is finished before they make their guesses.

Pica Fermé Nada

Begin by asking a student to think of a number with an agreed-upon number of digits (based on the age and skill level of the children playing). The student writes the number on a piece of paper, which she shows to you and then puts aside until the end of the activity.

On chart paper or a board, write a blank for each digit of the number: for example, _ _ _ for a three-digit number. Going around the circle, students try to figure out the number by suggesting three-digit numbers. For each suggestion, indicate how close it is to the mystery number using this code:

- Pica (P) means the numeral is in the mystery number but is in the wrong place.
- Fermé (F) means the numeral and place are correct.
- Nada (N) means the numeral is not in the mystery number at all.

For example, if the mystery number is 386 and someone suggests 365, write "365 — F P N."

Then the next person in the circle suggests a number based on this information, asking classmates for help if he'd like. Anyone who wants to pass may do so.

The activity continues until someone is ready to name the number—and explain the thinking that solved the mystery.

VARIATION ▪ Write the Pica, Fermé, and Nada symbols with no direct relationship to the placement of the numerals in the suggested number. For example, if the mystery number is 386 and a student suggests 365, you might write "N F P." If another student suggests 357, you might write "N F N." Students may welcome the extra challenge posed by the random placement of the symbols.

Scientific Pros and Cons

Students find a partner (or you assign partners). Distribute a sheet of paper and a pencil to each pair. Name a scientific venture they've been studying (such as bioengineering crops, introducing wolves or coyotes to control deer populations, or using alternative energy such as solar) and let them know that they'll have a chance to think about the pros and cons of this venture.

Give partners one minute to list pros of the venture. Then ring a chime and have them list cons. After a minute, ring the chime again and bring everyone back into the circle. Partners then share one pro and one con with the class.

Speed Ball

With everyone sitting or standing in a circle, call out a student's name and quickly toss the ball to her. She catches it, holds it for just a second as she calls out another student's name, and tosses the ball to him. She then turns her thumb up to indicate she's had a turn. Continue in this way until everyone has had a chance to toss and to catch.

Before the activity, it's important to establish and then review safety parameters such as throwing underhand, throwing toward the torso rather than the head, and throwing gently.

Group Activities to Try

Take Sides

Make up a list of contrasting statements about students' preferences—for example, "I love to sleep late" and "I love to get up early" or "I like to be with big groups" and "I like to be with one friend." With students standing in a line down the middle of the circle area, call out a pair of statements. Students for whom the first statement is true move to the left; students for whom the second statement is true move to the right. Students who don't feel strongly about either statement stay where they are. Continue calling out statements until everyone has moved a few times. Finish with a statement that's true of everyone in the class: "If you're in the sixth grade, find a place to sit down in our circle."

Telegraph

Students stand in a circle, hold hands, and close their eyes. The first student (or the teacher) chooses a nonverbal message, such as three quick, gentle hand squeezes, and sends it to the next child. He then sends the message to the next child, and so on around the circle. After the message goes around the whole circle, the last child explains verbally what it was. The message can also be sent in both directions at once until one child receives it from both sides.

What Are You Doing?

A student goes to the center of the circle and pantomimes a simple action such as brushing her hair. The next student in the circle approaches the hair-brusher and asks, "What are you doing?" The hair-brusher responds by saying something completely different, such as "I'm washing the floor," and then resumes her place in the circle. The person who asked now pretends that he is washing the floor. The next student in the circle approaches the floor-washer and asks, "What are you doing?" This goes on until everyone in the circle has had a chance to pantomime an action.

Zip, Zap, Pop

A student begins by placing his right or left hand on top of his head so his fingers are pointing to the student on his right or left, and saying "Zip." The student who receives the Zip can either pass it on to the next student in the circle, or place his hand under his chin, pointing back toward the student who passed him the Zip, and say "Zap," or he can point at someone across the circle and say "Pop." Continue until everyone has been zipped, zapped, or popped.

Zoom

The person who begins the activity says "Zoom!" and turns his head quickly to a neighbor on either the right or left. That person passes the Zoom to the next person, and so on around the circle. You can challenge the group to go faster and use a stopwatch to time them.

VARIATION ▪ Explain that the word "Eek!" stops the Zoom and makes it reverse direction. For the next round, allow one Eek and then in subsequent rounds increase the number of Eeks allowed. Remind children that the goal is to get the Zoom passed all the way around the circle. If only a few children have had a chance to say "Eek!" you can end the activity by having everyone say "Eek!" together.

Morning Message

A LETTER TO THE CLASS

The group activity finished, third grade teacher Ms. Alberti gets the class ready to read the morning message she has written to them. She divides the children into two groups and then directs their attention to the chart on an easel next to her. "We'll read alternate sentences by groups," she says. She points to the salutation. "Group one, you're on!"

When the students have read the entire message, Ms. Alberti reads the examples that students wrote on the chart before the meeting started: "Coffee, corn, popcorn, peanuts . . ."

She pauses and then asks, "What do you notice about the different seeds and foods made from seeds that we eat?"

"It's a long list," responds a student.

"Some we eat raw and some we eat cooked."

March 10, 2014

Hello, Botanists!
We have been learning about seeds.
Did you know that we eat many different types of seeds and foods made from seeds?

In the space below, write a seed we eat or a food made from seeds.
HINT: Look at the tray on the table.

coffee   CORN
Popcorn Peanuts

Sincerely,
Ms. Alberti

"We eat seeds all the time," another student says.

"You're right, we do," Ms. Alberti says. "Put your thumb up if you ate a seed or a seed-food for breakfast." She pauses while thumbs go up. "Now, turn to your partner and brainstorm a list of seeds or foods made from seeds that are often breakfast foods."

A lively hum fills the room. After a few minutes, Ms. Alberti gets the students' attention. "Today, during lunch," she says, "notice if you're eating any seeds or foods made from seeds. This afternoon, during science, we'll add to our list."

PURPOSES AND REFLECTIONS

Morning message provides information and academic reinforcement through a message written by the teacher each day. Students read the message as they enter the room and follow any instructions on it before Morning Meeting begins. Later, the message serves as the basis for the last component of Morning Meeting. During that component, teacher and students read the message, and the teacher engages the students in discussion based on its content.

The content and format of the message change as children get older, and so do the ways in which students interact with the message before and during the meeting. The methods and purposes of morning message, however, stay the same.

Purposes of Morning Message

- Builds community through shared written information

- Develops and reinforces language arts, math, and other academic skills in a meaningful and interactive way

- Eases the transition into the rest of the day and builds students' excitement about the day's learning

Morning message builds community through shared written information

Often teachers write their messages in the form of a letter: "Dear Room 22 Students," "Good morning, Friendly Workers," "Hello, Multiplying Mathematicians!" the letters may begin. From the opening salutations, students are addressed as a group and reminded of their membership in the classroom community.

Each message focuses primarily on one topic, with content that is relevant to all students. As teachers compose their messages to the class, they consider students' development, skills, and interests, and what is happening in the classroom. Sometimes, as in the opening vignette, content is drawn from the academic curriculum; other times the message emphasizes social aspects of classroom life.

Sometimes students respond to a question in the message by writing or drawing right on the message. Other times students simply read and think about the message before the meeting. But no matter what the content and format, students begin their day engaging with a shared written communication in an inclusive experience—the message pertains to all and we expect all to read and use it.

Morning message develops and reinforces language arts, math, and other academic skills in a meaningful and interactive way

The daily use of a written morning message provides an opportunity to practice a range of academic skills.

For younger children: A focus on literacy skills

For younger children, who are learning to read and write, the focus is often on literacy skills. The sentence structures and message formats are deliberately predictable and repetitious and teachers include frequent picture cues and familiar sight vocabulary, with only the topic changing from day to day. "Today is Monday. We will paint." or "Today is November 16. We will count in 2's in math." These simple sentence patterns, to which even the youngest quickly become accustomed, teach letter and number recognition, sight words, word families, and spelling and language patterns.

Students read the message upon arrival in the classroom.
During Morning Meeting, the teacher uses the message to do
a quick activity that offers challenges but allows success.

As students' abilities grow, teachers might include one or two sentences at the end of the message that use a new word or sentence structure, encouraging students to develop and practice strategies for independent reading of unfamiliar language. By looking to the day's activities or curriculum for the content of these sentences, teachers give children a taste of vocabulary they will see later in the day and help them transition into the day's learning: "We will use watercolors." "We will talk about our spider today."

Teachers may also include in their messages news or reminders about the day: "Bring your writing to Morning Meeting and be ready to share your opening sentence," or "Chandra's dad will cook with us today."

During the morning message portion of Morning Meeting, the teacher asks questions or plays quick games based on the information on the chart. For example:

- Who can find the letter "t"?
- Who can find two letters that go together and make the sound "ba"?
- Who can make a number sentence for the number five?
- Who can name something in our room that we have five of?

For older children: More complex and varied content

Although morning messages are not intended for introducing new content or skills, they do offer many opportunities for older children to practice a range of academic skills they've been introduced to and are working on. Teachers will often include content-area vocabulary for review or provide models for the type of writing students will encounter in their reading. They might insert deliberate punctuation errors for students to find and fix or math problems to solve.

In schools where upper grade students change classes, teachers can look to team members for academic ideas for the message. For example, the team members could rotate responsibilities for coming up with an academic challenge that can be used in every classroom. Or the team can write the messages collaboratively, focusing on math on Mondays, language arts on Tuesdays, and so forth. "What a lot we have learned about different ecosystems!" one teacher writes. "Think of a polyhedron before Morning Meeting and prepare a statement about it to share when we gather together," writes another teacher to a group studying three-dimensional figures.

Often teachers include an item that helps students learn about each other. "Who has a birthday this month?" "What's your favorite season?" "What book are you reading this week?" Teachers might include items that collect data about the class. For example, one message includes a chart listing sports (along with a "don't like any sport" column) and asks students to "Sign your name under your favorite sport." In the meeting itself, the class will discuss the data gathered and different ways they might graph it. Teachers may also take a moment to invite students who signed their name under "don't like any sport" to tell the class what non-sport hobby they like.

Messages to older students have more complex and varied content to match their maturity and skill level.

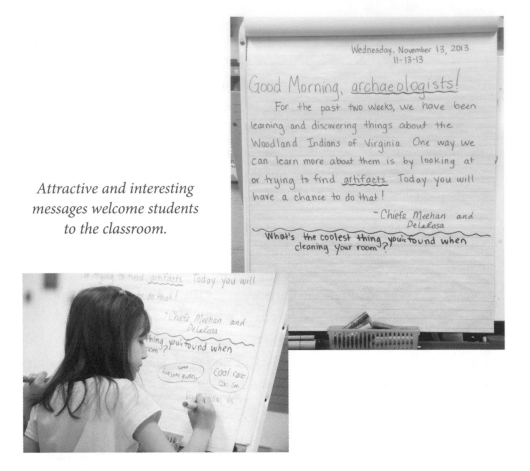

Attractive and interesting messages welcome students to the classroom.

Morning message eases the transition into the rest of the day and builds students' excitement about the day's learning

Seeing an attractive and interesting message waiting at the beginning of the day is one way students know that their teacher is ready for them, has thought about the day, and is welcoming them to it. Of course, teachers use the message to supplement, rather than replace, greeting students and checking in with them face-to-face as they enter the classroom in the morning.

Not only does the message help welcome students to the classroom, but the information in the message prepares them for the day's learning and events and helps them reflect on the learning and events of previous days. The message draws students in as it invites them to begin participating even before Morning Meeting: "List one fact you know about Sojourner Truth." "Draw a food that you saw on our trip to the store yesterday." "Can you find a spelling mistake or two in this message?"

During the morning message portion of Morning Meeting, the lively discussions and students' interaction with the message as a group help teachers send students into the rest of the day feeling engaged and capable, reassured about what they know and can do.

Highlights of Morning Message

- Includes a written message that welcomes and greets students as they enter the room

- Adds predictability and structure to morning arrival time

- Gets students excited about the day's learning

- Lets students know that the teacher has prepared for the day and is ready for them, which helps them feel safe and cared for

- Affords a fun and interactive way to review and practice eading, writing, math, and other skills

- Conveys that reading is a valuable way to get needed information

- Builds community through shared written information

- Provides a "warm-up" for the day's activities

- Eases the transition from Morning Meeting to the rest of the day
---

Morning Message

You may want to browse through the Sample Morning Messages section starting on page 190 before reading further.

GETTING STARTED

Introduce morning message slowly

As with other components of Morning Meeting, simplicity is best at first. Begin with simple messages and straightforward ways of reading them and then slowly build challenge and complexity as students are ready. On the first day of school, you might have a welcoming message written and posted in the meeting circle. When you get to the morning message part of the meeting, point to the message and let students know that every day they will find a message from you that they should read before the meeting and that they will use during and after the meeting as well. Over the next few days, model and practice various ways of reading and interacting with the message when students arrive in the morning.

I have often made a point of standing by the message chart during arrival time in the first week or so, greeting students and, if needed, providing some extra support in reading the message.

During those early days, when you get to the morning message portion of the meeting, you could read the message aloud with younger students, pointing to each word as you read. With older students, begin with choral reading for the irst few days. When students are comfortable with choral reading, begin to vary the ways you read the message from day to day—for example, the class might echo you or a classmate line by line, different groups might read different paragraphs, and so forth.

Plan the logistics of the message

You'll need to choose a prominent spot for the message so that it greets students as they enter the room. Be sure to choose a spot that won't interrupt early morning traffic flow when several children are clustered together, reading or responding to the message. Keeping the message in the same spot every morning helps make it part of the classroom routine.

Many teachers like to use a chart stand and easel paper for their message. In most

*The teacher places the message in a prominent spot
so that it greets students as they enter the room.*

rooms, this makes the message easier to physically move and incorporate into the meeting circle. Using paper and markers also eliminates the risks of smudges and erasures and allows you to save the chart and post it after the meeting. Some teachers put old charts in the class library for students to read during language arts or send the charts home with individual children on a rotating basis.

Because of the cost of chart paper, some teachers prefer to use dry erase boards. The boards work well in the moment but don't allow the teacher to save the message for later use. To address this, some teachers take digital pictures of the message each day and save the pictures for later use.

Still other teachers like to use an interactive whiteboard to write and post their message. They can save each day's message and print out a booklet of messages at the end of the year. If you're thinking about using this option, keep in mind that making the message part of the circle is important and that doing so may be a challenge when using a big screen.

Regardless of the medium you choose, what matters most is that the message content is relevant to the current life of the classroom and that students can easily interact with the message.

Tailor content, format, and activities to your particular class

Part of what makes a morning message of real interest to students is its pertinence to the classroom life of a particular group at a particular time. To be real and immediate, our messages must be specific to each day and class.

With younger groups in which most students are not yet fluent readers, even the predictable parts of the message are specific to the day, including such information as the date, the day's line leader, or a sentence about the weather. Additional content usually springs from current activities: "We will work with clay today" or "Look at our egg before Morning Meeting" or "Draw a food you like."

Morning Message Topics

Here are some things to consider when deciding on the content of each day's message.

- *Is it current?* Focusing on current work or building on work from previous days sets the stage for the day ahead.
- *Is it inclusive?* Every message should speak to all class members. All students should see themselves mirrored in the message.
- *Is it engaging?* The most effective topics are those that interest all students. Varying topics from day to day and using examples drawn from classroom life can help keep student interest high.

Here's a starter list of possible message topics:

- A plant or animal the class is observing
- An activity the class will be doing that day, such as going to a special or on a field trip
- The class pet
- Current events
- Favorites (numbers, books, games, and so on)
- Healthy foods and other healthy habits
- Memories or predictions
- Riddles, puns, and word plays
- Writing Workshop topics or any content the class is studying

---

When teaching older students with established reading skills, teachers have room for more variation in format, but the information should still derive from classroom activities and interests and should still be particular to the day. Perhaps it's World Series time and excitement is high; the message might feature a math problem involving statistics from yesterday's game. In another room, a seventh grade teacher writes the question "Do you know what today is?" and then includes historical facts about the date, followed by open-ended questions. Down the hall, a fifth grade teacher uses a new vocabulary word every day in the message, being sure to choose a word relevant to what students will be working on that day. She uses the word in a sentence and then challenges the students to figure out the meaning by using context clues.

Classroom community issues can also make good topics. Is a new student joining the class? You might prompt students to think about ways they can welcome her. Are students getting sloppy with cleanup after science experiments? Include a thinking question that helps them evaluate cleanup procedures. Were there problems during recess yesterday? The message might direct students to be prepared to share at Morning Meeting one way they can help make recess go more smoothly today.

Keep messages focused

Particularly in older grades, teachers are sometimes tempted to make the message comprehensive, squeezing in just one more thing students really ought to be thinking about, one more type of spelling error for them to find. This can get overwhelming, both for the students who read and act on the information and for the teacher who creates it.

Remember—the purposes of the morning message component are to welcome and greet students, to orient them and get them excited about their day, and to use the written format of the message for a quick "warm-up" skill-builder. Resist the temptation to launch into a spelling lesson based on an error students didn't catch or to list everything students will need to know about tomorrow's field trip.

Instead, file away the spelling error for a mini-lesson before writing time later in the week; then perhaps in the following week feature some examples of words with that spelling pattern in the morning message. And if the field trip requires substantial reminders, a separate field trip meeting in the afternoon is in order.

*Morning message provides a transition
to the rest of the day.*

Morning message, coming at the end of Morning Meeting, serves as a transition into the rest of the day. We want students to leave the meeting sensing their competence and feeling equipped to navigate their day. It's important, therefore, that these last few minutes of the meeting be well paced, calm, and uncluttered.

It's also helpful to keep the message visually, as well as informationally, clear and focused. Use just one color for most of the text and another, brighter color for highlighting a word or two or adding a simple decoration. Using many colors is cheerful but can also be overly stimulating.

Another way to keep the message focused is to avoid using the body of the message for announcements or reminders, such as "Put your writing journal in the basket on my table." Instead, set these aside in a bubble at the top or bottom of the message.

Finally, avoid posting the schedule for the day on the message—including the schedule each day can dilute the impact of the message. Although this information is important, write it in a separate place.

Decide which message elements to use

Following are elements often found in morning messages.

Greeting

A salutation or heading opens the message. Many teachers use a letter salutation such as "Dear Second Graders" or "Good morning, Focused Workers!" No matter what the choice of words, the greeting is friendly in tone and tells students, "This message is written especially for you! Come and read it!"

Date

You can date the message in various ways. For young children, using a consistent, predictable format is usually best. Teachers of emergent readers might begin with very simple structures, first writing "Today is [day of the week]" to teach the days of the week. They would then add statements about the month and the date, building to "Today is Monday, March 31, 2014."

As children acquire calendar skills and learn the days of the week and the names of the months, some teachers leave parts of the date blank and have the group fill them in during Morning Meeting.

In messages for more experienced readers, the date is usually located in a corner, as it would be in a letter. Students can benefit from seeing this information in a variety of formats: with and without abbreviations, or in "shorthand" such as 3/31/2014.

Body of the message

With the exception of very beginning readers, students should be able to read and understand at least parts of the message before Morning Meeting, either independently or with assistance from a classmate. Craft the reading level of your message with this in mind. In general, keep the language simple at the beginning of the year and increase the complexity as students are able to handle more sophisticated reading challenges. And throughout the year, continue to keep each message focused on one topic.

Related interactive tasks

The message may conclude with a question to think about or a simple activity for students to complete before the meeting starts. Such interactive tasks are most effective when they go hand in hand with the body of the message, inviting students to interact in some way with what they've just read. For example, "Look for 'ing' words in this message and be ready to point to them." Or "Find all of our word wall words in the message. Be ready to share them in our meeting."

Keep in mind that the message is a place for quick warm-ups and skill practice. The tasks that work best are those that everyone in the group will be able to complete quickly, independently, and successfully.

Closing and signature

Many teachers who write messages in letter format use a closing that's in a respectful and professional voice, such as "Sincerely," or "Your teacher," followed by their name or signature. Some teachers conclude with an encouraging phrase, such as "Let's have a great learning day!" or "Do your best!" The choice depends on what feels right for you and makes sense for a particular class.

Working with the message

Morning message gains its power from the interactions it generates—teacher communicating with students and students communicating with one another as they read the message, independently and as a group, and complete any related tasks. For this reason it's important to consider how you'll have students work with the message.

Before Morning Meeting

For most classes, the general expectation is that students will read the message and do any interactive tasks before Morning Meeting begins. Because students typically have several jobs to complete upon arrival in the classroom in the morning, it's important to teach the expectations for working with the message explicitly. Should they put away their backpacks and lunches, sign in, and then go over to read and interact with the message? Should they read and interact with the message before turning to their morning math challenge? Answer these questions clearly for yourself, and then teach the routine to the class.

When you introduce a new interactive task for students to do, such as using tally marks, filling in a Venn diagram, or putting data on a graph, be sure to model and practice it before asking students to do the task independently.

During Morning Meeting

In most classes, teachers begin the morning message component by leading the class in reading the message aloud. To keep things interesting, vary the way you read the message from day to day. Choral reading, line-by-line "echo" reading, and teacher or individual student reading can all work well. So can reading at different volumes or with different intonations. Keep in mind that students are generally more engaged with the message when they're reading it aloud, so limit the number of days when you have just one student read the message. (See the box "Ways to Read Morning Messages as a Class" on page 184 for more ideas.)

After reading the message, the class briefly discusses or works with the message in a way that expands on its content. For example, students might explore thinking questions posed in the message, comment on the message content, engage in skill practice embedded in the message, or make observations about what classmates wrote in the interactive portion of the message.

After Morning Meeting

Many teachers leave the message on display for the rest of the school day. This allows students to continue adding ideas. The message might also be used during lessons. A message that asks "What do you know about salmon?" might be posted on a wall so that students can add answers for the duration of their salmon study. Over time, the document becomes a testament to the class's learning.

Sometimes teachers will send message charts home with students on a rotating basis. I remember one parent telling me that she peeked into her son's room one evening. He had the day's message chart taped to his wall and was reading it

Morning Message

Ways to Read Morning Messages as a Class

- Choral read

- Read in different voices (whisper, spooky, loud, soft)

- Take turns: Divide group in half; one half reads a sentence (or paragraph) while the other listens; switch back and forth

- Echo read: Teacher or a student reads a sentence; rest of class echo-reads same sentence

- Have everyone read silently; then call on one student to paraphrase

- Pantomime read: Choose several words from the message, brainstorm ways to antomime them, and then read the message together, inserting those actions at the appropriate spots

- Chant or sing the message to a familiar tune

- Add sound effects for punctuation marks

- Say the salutation in another language, including American Sign Language

- Clap the beats for words with two or more syllables

aloud, using a ruler to point to each word. I smiled as I thought about the power of Morning Meeting extending beyond the classroom walls.

Some teachers make a class book of the messages each month and keep the books in their class library for students to read. Others save messages for a year and then use them as part of year-end assessment projects. When the messages are spread out in a large space, they provide a powerful visual story of the year's learning.

(For more suggestions on message content and how to work with messages during Morning Meeting, see *80 Morning Meeting Ideas for Grades K–2* by Susan Lattanzi Roser and *80 Morning Meeting Ideas for Grades 3–6* by Carol Davis, published by Northeast Foundation for Children.)

Morning message responsibilities

In implementing and assessing morning message, keep the following general responsibilities in mind.

Teachers' Responsibilities

- Prepare the message before students arrive.

- Model neat handwriting and correct grammar and punctuation in the written message (unless you're deliberately embedding errors for students to correct).

- Incorporate current curriculum into the message and any related interactive tasks.

- Vary the kinds of skills required in related interactive tasks.

- Select an appropriate format for reading the message during the meeting and vary the format regularly.

- Choose individual students to unscramble, decode, find errors, etc., while still keeping the whole group involved.

Students' Responsibilities

- Read the message upon entering the room.

- Follow any directions in the message.

- Read or follow along with the reading of the message during Morning Meeting.

- Participate in discussion or work based on the message before or during Morning Meeting.

FINE TUNINGS

Q **Students really like reading the morning message, but I find it hard to keep thinking of new things to write each day. I feel like it's taking me more time than it should to prepare the message.**

ANSWER ▪ You have lots of company, particularly among teachers of students in intermediate and upper grades. The predictable sentence starters and additional sentence or two that are just right for primary students are not challenging enough for older students.

Remember the recommendation from the Getting Started section about using the daily life of the classroom as a springboard for your message. Look to your ongoing curriculum and to your general observations and knowledge of your class for ideas rather than trying to think of fascinating, original tidbits. Do your students adore jokes and riddles? Are codes really fun for them right now? Are they all excited about the upcoming basketball season?

Some teachers have found that having a different but predictable topic for each day of the week helps them vary the content of their messages while removing the stress of total invention. Monday's message might always feature a question or tally about weekend activities, Tuesday's message might pose a math problem, Wednesday's might have a literacy focus, and Thursday's a topic from the social curriculum, such as how to take care of a guest teacher. To end the week, you could choose something from another content area or a current event.

Q **I have a class of twenty-seven sixth graders. We often don't have time for more than a quick reading of the message, particularly if our group activity has really grabbed the students. What can I do?**

ANSWER ▪ It's fine to vary the time spent on each meeting component based on your judgments about your class and what works for them—just be careful that the same component, such as morning message, doesn't always get cut short.

Some decisions about time variations happen on the spot: Perhaps a particularly riveting sharing prompts a deeper-than-usual exchange of questions, answers, and comments, and the teacher judges that it's worth cutting into group activity and message time to allow this fruitful conversation.

Other times, teachers know in advance that they'll need extra time for a particular meeting component and plan to shorten other components. Perhaps group activity needs to go a bit longer than usual because the teacher wants to introduce a new word game. Or perhaps the sharing component needs more time for students to share the models of solar-powered appliances they've been building in science. In such cases, an awareness of pacing will allow enough time for the group to fully engage in each component while not letting things drag or causing the meeting to extend beyond thirty minutes. However, while being flexible, teachers should keep in mind the purposes and elements of each component of Morning Meeting and make sure that all are encompassed over time—but not necessarily in each meeting.

Morning Message

Q **There are several ELL students in my classroom. Are there special considerations I should keep in mind when I write the messages and plan for morning message time?**

ANSWER ▪ The morning message is a wonderful tool for developing literacy for ELL students. Here are some ideas and caveats:

- Enlist the help of an ELL teacher or coach. For example, you could give the message to the ELL teacher to review with the student(s) before the meeting.

- To build vocabulary, stop frequently when reading the message aloud to ask students the definition of words.

- Use print rather than cursive when writing the message. Reading cursive can be challenging for students just beginning to read English.

- Be wary of embedding deliberate mistakes for students to correct in the message. Students with limited English proficiency may be confused, thinking the mistakes are actually correct renderings.

Q It's the middle of the year and very few of my students are reading and interacting with the message before the meeting. What should I do to increase participation?

ANSWER ▪ The first thing to do is to step back and review your messages and plans for working with them. Do they reflect classroom life? Are the interactive tasks varied? Have you included content that will engage students?

When I first began doing Morning Meeting, I also noticed a mid-year lull in morning message participation, and I decided to ask the students about it. I told them that I'd noticed that only a few of them were reading and responding to the message each day. Why might that be? The honest and articulate nine- and ten-year-olds responded very kindly but matter-of-factly. "Well, Mrs. Davis, to be honest, they're not so interesting to read—they basically say the same thing every day. We know we have music on Thursdays and art on Fridays."

Aha! I had started using the messages mostly for announcements and reminders. I wasn't putting enough thought into making them interesting and engaging for students, just like a good book. If I wanted students to read the message, I needed to vary what I did each day and put something in each message that would capture their attention.

As I probed a bit more, I discovered that some students had difficulty reading the message independently. So, along with making them more engaging, I needed to simplify the language to be sure that they appealed to readers at a variety of levels.

Finally, I noticed that some students struggled with organization skills and just plain forgot to read the message or ran out of time for it because they got caught up in other morning tasks.

To address the issue of varied reading levels and to help students with organization, I started using "Message Partners." I carefully considered students' strengths and challenges in reading, focus, and organizational skills and paired them up accordingly so that a student strong in one area, such as reading, was paired with someone who might struggle with reading. Or I would pair a student who had competent organizational skills with a student who had trouble getting tasks done. Each morning, the partners would get together and read and interact with the message.

Q **Students arrive at different times at my school. How do I make sure all have a chance to work with the message before Morning Meeting?**

ANSWER ▪ One way to deal with this issue is to prioritize morning tasks, emphasizing that reading and interacting with the message should be the first task accomplished.

Another idea is to have early arrivers assist late arrivers in working with the message. You can pair early and late arrivers (this can be one consideration as you assign "Message Partners"—see the preceding Q&A). To save time, the early arriver can summarize the message and explain the related interactive task (if you've included one) or help with tasks such as turning in homework or hanging up a backpack. This gives the late arriver more time to read and interact with the message.

Morning Message

SAMPLE MORNING MESSAGES

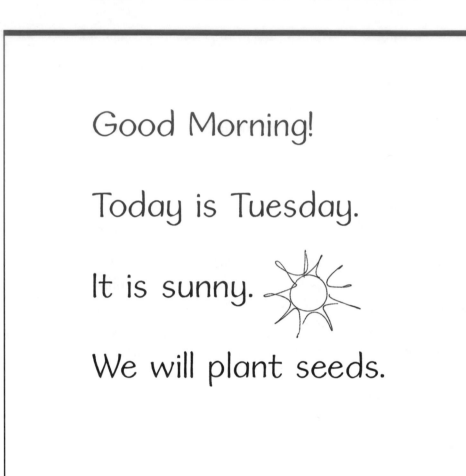

K

Messages

Good Morning!

Today is Tuesday.

It is sunny.

We will plant seeds.

Ideas for working with the message

- Have students find and underline word wall words that are in the message.

- Echo read the message.

- Help children look ahead to their day with questions like:

  ↪ What kinds of seeds do you know about or have you seen before?

  ↪ What kinds of seeds do you think we might plant in our classroom this afternoon?

Sample
Morning
Messages

Ideas for working with the message

- Read the message to the class and then choral read.
- Ask a few questions about students' predictions:
  - What do you think happened to Junie B. Jones's gloves?
  - Where do you think she might find them?
  - What do you think she will do when she finds them?
  - Why are those gloves so important to her?

1st

**Grade
Messages**

Good Morning!

Today is Tuesday, October 21st.

We will think about soil.

Look at the soil in the plants in our room. Be ready to share something you notice or know about soil.

Ideas for working with the message

- Choral read the message.
- Invite a few students to share their noticings.

Today is Thursday, April 17th.

Anna is first today.

We will have time to play
our song in music today!

What is your favorite song?
What is your favorite instrument?
Be ready to share.

Ideas for working with the message

- Choral read and add in sound effects for each type of punctuation.

- Ask children to name the punctuation signs they see in the message.

- Invite children to make the sound of the instrument they've named.

Grade Messages

November 6, 2014

Dear Math Experts,

How many buttons do we all have today? We'll look at our graph during math later this morning.

Count the buttons on your clothing. Then put a sticker on our line graph to show how many buttons you have:

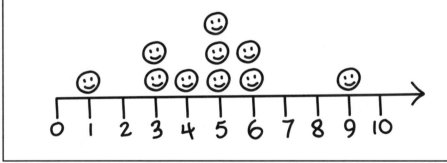

Ideas for working with the message

- Echo read the message, line by line.

- Reflect on the data students provided. Here are some questions you could ask:

  ➥ What is the greatest number of buttons someone has?

  ➥ What is the least?

  ➥ What number do you think is in the middle?

  ➥ What are some ways we could add up all the buttons we have?

Tuesday, May 14, 2015

Dear Geologists:

You have learned a lot about how wind and water can change the shape of land. Can you think of ways we could <u>prevent</u> wind and water from reshaping the land? Hmm. Talk about your ideas with a partner.

Write one idea below (if someone already wrote your idea put a check mark by it):

tall fence ✓

thick bushes

Ideas for working with the message

- Brainstorm ways students can use their bodies to show wind or water.

- Choral read the message. Whenever you get to the word "wind" or "water," students show their ideas from the brainstorming.

- Read the ideas that students wrote. Ask a few students to explain their thinking and add any new ideas.

3rd

**Grade
Messages**

Wednesday, Nov. 12, 2014

Dear Friendly Workers,

We have been practicing giving compliments to each other. Today in Writer's Workshop we will be doing peer conferences. What might be something that you could compliment your writing partner about? Write your idea below.

Your teacher, Mrs. Davis

Ideas for working with the message

- Choral read the message.

- Have a brief discussion about compliments. Possible questions:

  ↪ Why do we give compliments?

  ↪ What are some things to remember when giving a compliment to someone?

  ↪ How does it feel to receive a compliment? What might you do when you receive a compliment?

4/1/2015

Hello, Tricksters, and Happy April Fool's Day!

It is believed that April Fool's Day began in France in the 1560's. At that time New Year's Day was April 1st. Then the king changed it to January 1st. Those who continued to celebrate the new year in April were called "April Fools."

Have you ever played a trick on someone on April Fool's Day? Place a tally mark below:

YES	NO

I will definitely be on my toes today!
Mrs. Roser

Sample Morning Messages

Ideas for working with the message

- Divide the group in two and alternate reading the message sentence by sentence.

- Possible questions to use to facilitate discussion:

  - Where else can we go to find out facts about holidays?

  - When is trick-playing fun for everyone? When might it hurt someone's feelings? How could we take care of each other?

  - Why might it be important to be able to laugh at ourselves sometimes?

4th

Grade Messages

Wednesday, November 19, 2014

Good Morning, Space Explorers!

Did you know that gravity is stronger on Earth than it is on the moon? In fact, things weigh only 1/6 as much on the moon. What would you be able to do if you weighed so much less? What wouldn't you be able to do? Be ready to share during our meeting.

Ideas for working with the message

- Have students silently read the message. Ask for a student to paraphrase the message.

- Help students understand "1/6" if needed. Ask volunteers to share answers to the questions and their reasoning.

2/10/15

Dear Awesome Artists,

Your illustrations for our class read-aloud books are fantastic! They show such a rich variety of ideas and feelings about the book. I would like to display all of your illustrations for everyone to see. Let's brainstorm some interesting ways that we might arrange this display. Be ready to share your ideas.

Have a great learning day!

Mrs. Hofmann

Ideas for working with the message

- Divide the class into two groups and alternate reading the message sentence by sentence.

- Have students talk with partners about ways to create a display. Invite some to share their ideas with the whole group.

- Ask for students' ideas about whether illustrations should be grouped by style, topic, or some other organizing characteristic.

September 26, 2014

Dear Friends of the Outdoors,

Before we start our new unit on nature, I am wondering . . . What is one thing you love about the great outdoors? Write it in a box below with your name.

WHAT I LOVE ABOUT NATURE:

QUOTE OF THE DAY:

"To me a lush carpet of pine needles or spongy grass is more welcome than the most luxurious Persian rug."   —HELEN KELLER

Ideas for working with the message

- Choral read the message.

- Have a few students read their response aloud and invite anyone who has a connection to it to give a "me too" signal.

- Lead a brief discussion about the quote and what students are most looking forward to learning about nature.

May 12, 2015

Dear **Amiable** Students,

I love reading so much that sometimes I worry that I read **excessively**! Do you think it's possible to read too much? Do you ever worry that you spend too much time doing just one thing?

Managing time well is a valuable skill. So, let's think about how we can **evaluate** our use of time. Write one way you can think of.

Your **affable** teacher, Mrs. Kimbell

Sample
Morning
Messages

Ideas for working with the message

- Discuss the meaning and pronunciation of the bolded words. You might ask, "Can you figure out the meaning of the words using context clues?"

- Brainstorm with students a quick gesture to use for each of the bolded words. Read the message together, doing the motion for each bolded word.

- Invite a few students to share their ideas for how to evaluate their use of time and how to use time more wisely.

Grade Messages

October 15, 2014

Good Morning, Journalists!

During our writing period today, we need to complete the preparation for our interviews so we will all be ready to record soon. I know many of you are looking forward to doing this final phase. We will talk about the following questions in meeting today. Bring your thoughts.

- What is the purpose of our interviews?

- How can we prepare for an interview?

- Write an interesting, useful, and appropriate interview question below:

Ideas for working with the message

- Invite a few students to share their process for coming up with a good interview question.

- Discuss other kinds of media that journalists sometimes include with their written interviews (sound clips, photos, video).

4/16/2015

Dear Historians,

Yesterday was so interesting as we delved into the Civil War period. In the boxes below, write one thing you learned about the North or the South or a question that arose from your homework reading last night.

NORTH	SOUTH
QUESTIONS ABOUT THE CIVIL WAR	

CHALLENGE:

Let's see how many **different** ideas we can collect from your reading!

—Mr. Shedd

Ideas for working with the message

- Take a look together at the learnings students wrote down. See if they want to add any other important learnings.

- Take a look together at the questions students have about the Civil War period. These could serve as the springboard for their work today in history. If you have time, discuss one or two of the questions. Brainstorm where to find answers.

9/25/2014

Welcome, Recyclers, to the Team Recycling Challenge!

We all know how important it is to recycle, right? But did you also know that recycling depends on companies wanting to reuse plastics, paper, and other materials to make new products?

Later today in science, we'll form product development teams. Each team will invent a new product that uses at least one recycled material. What can you do to help your team meet this challenge successfully? Write one idea here.

Give everybody a
turn to speak   Divide up responsibilities

Ideas for working with the message

- Use "Word Turns" (go around circle with each person reading just one word). Challenge the class to work as a group to read it as fluently as possible, as if one person is reading it.

- Invite students to briefly share what recycled products they or their families use.

- Ask students to read aloud their idea and discuss what makes teams successful. Encourage students to add any new ideas they think of to the message throughout the day.

March 12, 2015

Dear Class,

You've been working hard on your research into the Revolutionary War! Now it's time to think of creative ways to show what you've learned. Brainstorm some ideas and jot them down here.

I'm looking forward to hearing your creative ideas.
Mr. Sanchez

Ideas for working with the message

- Have students read the message to themselves silently, look at the ideas jotted down, and then discuss with partners:
  - More ideas to add to the list.
  - One idea they might be interested in and why.
- Invite volunteers to share with the whole group one thing they and their partners said.

October 29, 2014

Good Morning, Sports Fans!

I heard some of you talking about basketball yesterday. Here are some shooting statistics for some players of our city's basketball team in their last game. Make an educated guess at who had the highest and lowest percentage by simply looking at the numbers. Then calculate the percentages. (Work with a classmate if you'd like.) Bring your answers to Morning Meeting.

PLAYER	SHOTS TAKEN	SHOTS MADE
Jones	12	7
Stanton	9	3
Manning	14	8
Young	16	7

Ideas for working with the message

- Invite a student to read the message.

- Ask for volunteers to share their educated guesses along with their reasoning, and then their calculated answers.

- Ask the class if they agree with the calculations, redoing them together to verify.

February 5, 2015

Good Morning, Eighth Graders.

I have noticed how invested you all have been in our class discussions about bullying. It really does take all of us working together to make our school safe for everyone.

Last week we had a rich discussion about what actually is bullying behavior. Today we will begin talking about how we can be an ally to someone targeted by bullying. Be thinking about what it might look like and sound like to be an ally, what might be hard about being an ally, and what can help us be an ally even if it's hard. We will begin to share some ideas in meeting today.

Your ally, Mrs. Davis

Sample Morning Messages

Ideas for working with the message

- Begin a brief discussion about the meaning of the word "ally" to make sure everyone understands the meaning. For example, you might ask, "What is an ally? Where have you heard this word before?"

- Have students discuss with partners what might be hard about being an ally to a target of bullying and what can help them overcome those challenges. Have a few students share out.

Special Area
Messages

LIBRARY

November 3, 2014

Greetings, Researchers!

November is Aviation History Month. An aviator is someone who flies an airplane or other aircraft.

Thinking question: What resources might you use if you wanted to research famous aviators?

Idea for working with the message

- Ask for volunteers to share ideas about research resources. Use this to transition into a lesson on doing research.

MUSIC

April 25, 2015

Good morning, happy harmonizers!

Our spring concert is two weeks away!
We sure have learned a lot of songs
from around the world and have had fun
learning to sing in different languages.

What's one thing you want to work on
between now and the concert? Be ready
to share with a partner.

Ideas for working with the message

- Choral read the message (you could ask students to "harmonize" the phrase "happy harmonizers").

- Have students pair up to share thoughts about what they want to work on. Ask a few to share out with the whole group.

The Power of Morning Meeting

"Morning Meeting is a silent bulldozer in the field of school reform," proclaimed Maurice Sykes many years ago, when he was Deputy Superintendent for the District of Columbia school system. And it's true. When Morning Meeting is a regular part of a daily routine, it clears away the obstacles that impede children from feeling safe and engaged in school, creating the space for classroom members to take care of each other and to do their best learning. However, Morning Meetings do not just clear a space, they also help build what will fill that clearing.

Morning Meeting is not just a bulldozer, but also a crane, hoisting and setting into place the blocks of a new and sturdy foundation: Attentiveness, inquiry, kindness, respect, assertiveness, risk-taking, energy, and joy. Meeting after meeting, as members of the classroom community greet each other and share and play together, this foundation enables them to build a positive classroom, one within which students thrive.

With intangible constructions, unlike their counterparts of steel and concrete, it can be hard to measure the dimensions of our progress. It's slow, cumulative work, this building. But we listen and we watch and we see: which blocks are solidly interlocked into place and which are shaky and need shoring up. And from time to time, when we get to step back and observe, we are heartened.

Day after day, in schools all over America, teachers who use the approach described in this book begin the day with Morning Meetings that are safe, challenging, and joyful circles of learning. Are there moments when the orderliness teeters and the teacher has to redirect students? Moments when someone forgets what respectful listening looks like and needs reminding? Of course, for that's what daily school life is like: vision and aspiration, steps forward and regular stumbles when students need a hand to regain their footing and move ahead again. Still in every classroom that begins with Morning Meeting, students are engaged in learning and connecting with the people in the circle around them.

Morning Meeting is, on its surface, a simple and straightforward structure: everyone circled up beginning each day with four sequential components. The chapters in this book have described these components and the many ways in which they build social and academic skills as well as classroom community. All the skills that it teaches are essential to help children grow and develop into smart, principled, and caring adults. However, with Morning Meeting, as with many simple and straightforward designs, the impact of the whole is greater than the sum of its parts, and results in more than the acquisition of specific skills.

This edition comes at a time—as has been the case for many decades—when there is a pervasive sense of urgency in our country about whether students will be well prepared for high school, college, and the future they will face. And, as always, there are advocates for simply accelerating the pace of instruction, crowding more and more into the days of elementary school children—and their teachers. Fortunately there are also strong and respected voices reminding us how critical it is to foster deeper attributes that promote and sustain success: curiosity, persistence, and empathy, to name a few. These are some of the very attributes that Morning Meetings nurture and time used for them does not distract from, but rather fortifies, achievement. As one teacher said of Morning

Morning Meetings are safe, challenging, and joyful circles of learning.

Meeting, "Those tools, the simple strategies and clear structures, move us in the direction of profound goals. Sometimes we don't even know the full import of what's happening for a long time."

What we do know is this:

In the safe learning communities that Morning Meetings help build, students speak and listen to each other, they play and work together—day after day, year after year. Along with academic strengths, they develop a sense of who they are and what is of value. And they develop strong and respectful voices along with the skills to deploy those voices toward varied and positive ends: to inquire, to explain, to console, to assert, to stand up for a friend or a conviction. Wherever students journey and whatever joys and challenges their journeys bring, these abilities will serve them and the world they inhabit.

References

Bellanca, J., & Brandt, R. (Eds.). (2010). *21st century skills: Rethinking how students learn.* Bloomington, Indiana: Solution Tree.

Blum, R. W. (2005). A case for school connectedness. *Educational Leadership, 62*(7), 16–20. Retrieved from http://www.ascd.org/publications/educational leadership/apr05/vol62/num07/A-Case-for-School-Connectedness.aspx

CASEL (Collaborative for Academic, Social, and Emotional Learning). (n.d.). What is social and emotional learning? Retrieved from http://www.casel.org/ social-and-emotional-learning

Common Core State Standards Initiative. (2012). Retrieved from http://www.corestandards.org/ELA-Literacy/CCRA/SL

Durlack, J. A., Dymnicki, A. B., Schellinger, K. B., Taylor, R. D. & Weissberg, R. P. (2011). *The impact of enhancing students' social and emotional learning: A meta-analysis of school-based universal interventions.* Retrieved from http://casel.org/wp-content/uploads/Meta-Analysis-Child-Development-Full-Article1.pdf

Elias, M. J., Zins, J. E., Weissberg, R. P., Frey, K. S., Greenberg, M. T., Haynes, N. M., et al. (1997). *Promoting social and emotional learning: Guidelines for educators.* Alexandria, VA: Association for Supervision and Curriculum Development.

Goodson, B., & Layzer, C. (2009). *Learning to talk and listen: An oral language resource for early childhood caregivers.* Washington, DC: National Institute for Literacy.

Palmer, P. J. (1998). *The courage to teach: Exploring the inner landscape of a teacher's life.* San Francisco: Jossey-Bass.

Partnership for 21st Century Skills. (n.d.). Reimagining citizenship for the 21st century. Retrieved from http://www.p21.org/

Rogoff, B. (1990). *Apprenticeship in thinking: Cognitive development in social context*. San Francisco: Oxford University Press.

Sendak, M. *Chicken soup with rice*. (1962). New York: HarperTrophy.

Senge, P. M., Roberts, C., Ross, R. B., Smith, B. J., & Kleiner, A. (1994). *The fifth discipline fieldbook: Strategies and tools for building a learning organization*. New York: Currency Doubleday.

Zweirs, J., & Crawford, E. (2011). *Academic conversations: Classroom talk that fosters critical thinking and content understanding*. Portland, Maine: Stenhouse.

References

Further Resources

All of the Morning Meeting practices in this book come from or are consistent with *Responsive Classroom*®, an evidence-based elementary education approach associated with greater teacher effectiveness, higher student achievement, and improved school climate. This approach helps educators build competencies in four interrelated domains: engaging academics, positive community, effective management, and developmentally appropriate teaching. To learn more about the *Responsive Classroom* approach, see the following resources published by Northeast Foundation for Children and available from www.responsiveclassroom.org, 800-360-6332.

Morning Meeting

80 Morning Meeting Ideas for Grades K–2 by Susan Lattanzi Roser. 2012.

80 Morning Meeting Ideas for Grades 3–6 by Carol Davis. 2012.

Doing Language Arts in Morning Meeting: 150 Quick Activities That Connect to Your Curriculum by Jodie Luongo, Joan Riordan, and Kate Umstatter. February 2015.

Doing Math in Morning Meeting: 150 Quick Activities That Connect to Your Curriculum by Andy Dousis and Margaret Berry Wilson. 2010.

Doing Science in Morning Meeting: 150 Quick Activities That Connect to Your Curriculum by Lara Webb and Margaret Berry Wilson. 2013.

Morning Meeting Messages K–6: 180 Sample Charts from Three Classrooms by Rosalea S. Fisher, Eric Henry, and Deborah Porter. 2006.

99 Activities and Greetings: Great for Morning Meeting . . . and other meetings, too! by Melissa Correa-Connolly. 2004.

Doing Morning Meeting: The Essential Components DVD and viewing guide. 2004.

Sample Morning Meetings in a Responsive Classroom DVD and viewing guide. 2009.

Morning Meeting Professional Development Kit. 2008.

Child Development

Yardsticks: Children in the Classroom Ages 4–14, 3rd ed., by Chip Wood. 2007.

Child Development Pamphlets (based on *Yardsticks* by Chip Wood; in English or Spanish). 2005 and 2006.

Classroom Organization

Classroom Spaces That Work by Marlynn K. Clayton and Mary Beth Forton. 2001.

Effective Management

Interactive Modeling: A Powerful Technique for Teaching Children by Margaret Berry Wilson. 2012.

Teaching Children to Care: Classroom Management for Ethical and Academic Growth K–8, revised ed., by Ruth Sidney Charney. 2002.

What Every Teacher Needs to Know, K–5 series, by Mike Anderson and Margaret Berry Wilson. 2010–2011.

Engaging Academics

The Language of Learning: Teaching Children Core Thinking, Speaking, and Listening Skills by Margaret Berry Wilson. 2014.

Learning Through Academic Choice by Paula Denton, EdD. 2005.

The First Weeks of School

The First Six Weeks of School by Paula Denton and Roxann Kriete. 2000.

Movement, Games, Songs, and Chants

Closing Circles: 50 Activities for Ending the Day in a Positive Way by Dana Januszka and Kristen Vincent. 2012.

Energizers! 88 Quick Movement Activities That Refresh and Refocus by Susan Lattanzi Roser. 2009.

Positive Teacher Language

The Power of Our Words: Teacher Language That Helps Children Learn, 2nd ed., by Paula Denton, EdD. 2013.

Teacher Language for Engaged Learning: 4 Video Study Sessions. 2013.

Teacher Language Professional Development Kit. 2010.

Teaching Discipline

Responsive School Discipline: Essentials for Elementary School Leaders by Chip Wood and Babs Freeman-Loftis. 2011.

Rules in School: Teaching Discipline in the Responsive Classroom, 2nd ed., by Kathryn Brady, Mary Beth Forton, and Deborah Porter. 2011.

Teasing, Tattling, Defiance, and More: Positive Approaches to 10 Common Classroom Behaviors by Margaret Berry Wilson. 2013.

Teaching Discipline in the Classroom Professional Development Kit. 2011.

Solving Behavior Problems with Children

How to Bullyproof Your Classroom by Caltha Crowe. 2012.

Sammy and His Behavior Problems: Stories and Strategies from a Teacher's Year by Caltha Crowe. 2010.

Solving Thorny Behavior Problems: How Teachers and Students Can Work Together by Caltha Crowe. 2009.

Working with Families

Parents and Teachers Working Together by Carol Davis and Alice Yang. 2005.

Further Resources

Acknowledgments

From Roxann and Carol:

So many people's thoughts and work are incorporated into this book. Our own experiences over the past couple of decades, the experiences of scores of other educators, conversations with colleagues at Northeast Foundation for Children (NEFC), and conversations with those in the broader field of education are all reflected here.

Of course, no book about Morning Meeting would be complete without an expression of gratitude to the founders of NEFC—Marlynn Clayton, Ruth Charney, Jay Lord, and Chip Wood—and to many colleagues at NEFC's lab school and the public schools with whom NEFC engaged in the early years. The ideas behind Morning Meeting and the practices still at its core grew from their knowledge, passion, and hard work.

This book was a team effort. Specifically, we would like to thank:

Mary Beth Forton, for her encouragement and guidance in the early thinking about this revision. Mary Beth's thoughtfulness and clarity enriched both the product and the process of this work.

Lynn Bechtel, for her most able project management through every stage of this book. We appreciate her accessibility, patience, flexibility, and skill in blending the ideas, voices, and schedules of two authors.

Alice Yang, who provided skillful oversight and insight to all who were involved with this project.

Jim Brissette, for helping compile the "Ideas to Try" sections.

Elizabeth Nash, for her masterful copyediting.

Cathy Hess, for her meticulous proofreading.

Helen Merena, for a design that is beautiful: both familiar and fresh.

We would also like to thank the readers of this manuscript: Jane Aminatu Cofie-Raczko, Andrew Moral, Chris Hall, and Kristen Vincent, for their attention and range of perspectives.

From Roxann:

I would like to thank all the teachers and students who welcomed me into their Morning Meetings and shared their reflections. Thanks especially to the staff and students at International Charter School in Pawtucket, Rhode Island; Four Corners School in Greenfield, Massachusetts; and Stony Hill Elementary School in Wilbraham, Massachusetts. I went away from each visit inspired about the ways schools can be places both of nurture and of high achievement. Their practice—and that of thousands of others in schools across the country—helps enrich the ongoing evolution of Morning Meeting, keeping it relevant and powerful.

It was a pleasure and a privilege to share the authorship of this edition with Carol. Her experiences and deep understanding of teaching and learning infuse this edition with ideas that add immeasurably to it.

And, on a personal note, I want to thank my husband, Russ, and my family for their love and support in all that I do, including this project.

From Carol:

I was honored to co-author the third edition of *The Morning Meeting Book* with Roxann. I have always admired her vision, her keen insight, and her thoughtfulness about this important work.

I would like to thank all the teachers who have opened up their classrooms to me. In particular, I want to thank Martha Hanley and Pat Fekete for sharing ideas of how they adapted Morning Meeting to work within a departmentalized setting for older students.

Additionally, I would like to thank my colleagues Susan Roser and Mike Anderson, who helped me think through and sort out ideas; Marlynn Clayton, who first introduced me to Morning Meeting and coached me every step of the way in my work as a teacher and consultant; and Gretchen Bukowick, who supported and encouraged me throughout the writing.

During the writing of this book, my family and I moved from Michigan to Virginia. I would like to thank my amazing family, who rallied around me in this hectic time and gave me space to write. My parents, Larry and Honey Hofmann, and my sister and brother in-law Anne and Jason Regules helped keep my day-to-day family life going. And my husband, Tim, and our three children Riley, Brady, and Ruby offered unbelievable love, support, and encouragement—their hugs and cheers of "You can do it, Mom!" helped me immensely. Thank you for being there with me and for me every step of the way.

About the Authors

Roxann Kriete taught at both the elementary and secondary levels during her thirty-five-year career in education. She began working at Northeast Foundation for Children (NEFC) in 1985, retiring in 2011 after serving for ten years as NEFC's executive director. Roxann authored the previous editions of *The Morning Meeting Book* and co-authored *The First Six Weeks of School* (NEFC, 2000). In addition to revising *The Morning Meeting Book*, she has recently been writing a series of short stories.

Carol Davis has worked as a teacher, counselor, and consultant for grades K–8 for over twenty years. Currently, Carol is a professional development designer and *Responsive Classroom* consultant at NEFC. She is also the author of *80 Morning Meeting Ideas for Grades 3–6* and co-author of *Parents & Teachers Working Together* (NEFC, 2005).

Index

ABOUT THE PUBLISHER

Northeast Foundation for Children, Inc., a not-for-profit educational organization, is the developer of *Responsive Classroom*®, an evidence-based education approach associated with greater teacher effectiveness, higher student achievement, and improved school climate. *Responsive Classroom* practices help educators build competencies in four inter-related domains: engaging academics, positive community, effective management, and developmentally appropriate teaching. We offer the following resources for educators:

Professional Development Services

→ Workshops for teachers and administrators (locations around the country and on-site)

→ On-site consulting services to support implementation

→ Resources for site-based study

→ National conference for school and district leaders

Publications and Resources

→ Books and videos for teachers and school leaders

→ Professional development kits for school-based study

→ Website with extensive library of free articles: www.responsiveclassroom.org

→ Free newsletter for educators

→ The *Responsive*® blog, with news, ideas, and advice from and for educators

For details, contact:

Responsive Classroom®

Northeast Foundation for Children, Inc.
85 Avenue A, P.O. Box 718
Turners Falls, Massachusetts 01376-0718

800-360-6332   www.responsiveclassroom.org
info@responsiveclassroom.org